PRACTICAL

Ponds, Pools, Falls & Fountains

DON HARPER

W. Foulsham

London · New York · T...

D0234827

W. Foulsham & Company Limited
Yeovil Road, Slough, Berkshire, SL1 4JH

Cover photograph by Brigitte Thomas

ISBN 0-572-01700-6

Copyright © 1984 and 1992 W. Foulsham & Company Limited

Photoset in Great Britain by David John Services Ltd
and printed in Hong Kong

Contents

An established water garden can be a stunning sight.

Introduction

The inclusion of a pond in the garden will add another dimension for the gardener, as well as offering considerable potential for the naturalist. The scope is enormous, since water gardens can be devised to have a semi-wild appearance, or may be of a more formal design. They can be augmented with waterfalls or fountains, while fish may form the major feature or simply contribute to the overall scenery.

Brief history

The origins of water gardening can be traced back to ancient Egypt. Tomb murals and other evidence reveal that artificial ponds were a feature of gardens as long ago as 3000 BC. Water-lilies were probably cultivated in these ponds, with Rameses III having such 'Lotus flowers' growing alongside rushes about 1225 BC.

Further east, in China and Japan particularly, ponds became closely associated with Buddhist monasteries. Here other native Lotuses were favoured. It was common practice for the pools to be crossed by bridges, designed in the shape of a semi-circle. Their reflection in the water created the image of a complete circle to the observer. The tranquility of such surroundings inspired various Chinese writers to capture the scene in verse. The earth which had been dug out to create the pond was usually piled up nearby, and linked to the pool by a stream, with a building of some kind constructed on top of the hillock.

Similar designs prevailed in Japan, where water featured prominently in the layout of gardens, and had a symbolic role. Small bridges, islands, even miniature trees were used to create the effect of a cameo landscape.

The Romans viewed water gardens more prosaically, both as providing a decorative feature and also for irrigation purposes. Later, in medieval times, ponds became a common sight at

The giant water lily, *Victoria amazonia.*

monasteries, acting as a source of fresh fish for the table. Only during the Renaissance did the pond become appreciated again for its aesthetic qualities. Subsequently, a number of landscape architects were commissioned by wealthy patrons to design gardens which featured water.

This movement began in Italy, and one of the earliest examples at the Palazzo Vecchio, Florence includes a fountain, and a laughing cherub designed by the Italian sculptor del Verrocchio (1435-1488). Charles VII encouraged the trend in French gardens, after a visit to Italy. Spain, meantime, had previously become a centre for water gardens, while under Moorish occupation during the Middle Ages. Canals were the characteristic feature of these gardens and always formed the centre-piece of this introduced North African style.

This concept was later revived in Britain. At Chatsworth house in Derbyshire, a canal was set up to flow around the whole estate by diverting part of the River Derwent. Other embellishments, such as fountains, were included by the Frenchman Grelly, who was responsible for designing the layout. Water also played a major part in the design of gardens at other British stately homes, where it is still much in evidence today.

The influence of water-lilies

When the importation of water-lilies began in earnest during the latter part of the nineteenth century, water gardening became a very popular pursuit. Prior to this, some of the more delicate lilies had been persuaded to flower indoors in conservatory pools. It was at Chatsworth where the Giant Water-lily (*Victoria amazonia*) initially produced blooms under such conditions, and this was a notable triumph for the superintendent responsible, Joseph Paxton.

The first of the many hardy hybrids now seen today made their appearance during the 1880s. A whole range of colours, from the deepest shades of red through pink to yellow, were established in France, by M. Marliac. Dwarf varieties also attracted much attention.

A mature copper water-lily.

Ponds today

During recent years, the task of constructing a pond has been greatly simplified by the introduction of new materials, such as pond liners, so that it is no longer necessary to mix large amounts of concrete in order to produce a water-tight structure. Modern electronic apparatus, such as filters, pumps and lighting have greatly increased the scope of water gardening, and even a relatively small pond can enhance any garden. Considerable flexibility is now possible, and providing the initial site is chosen carefully, it is quite feasible to expand from a basic pond to create an area of flowing water, allowing the incorporation of different plants as well as other features such as waterfalls.

Ponds and their construction

Careful planning as a preliminary step is essential, irrespective of the size or type of pool you choose. Mistakes made once building is underway will be both expensive and frustrating to correct. There are various materials which can be used, and their potential advantages and drawbacks are considered in the latter part of the chapter. In the first instance, however, it will be important to decide on the positioning and design of the pond.

Siting

A bright location is best, in a spot where the sun's rays can fall on the water both morning and evening, yet affording some protection during the hottest part of the day. Such conditions are ideal for water-lilies as well as fish.

Under no circumstances is a site under trees to be recommended. Leaves will rapidly accumulate in the water during the autumn, polluting the pond. As these decay, the resulting gases may harm the fish during the winter, especially if the water freezes. Some shrubs, such as rhododendrons and holly, are directly poisonous to fish if leaves contaminate the water. Laburnum is a particular hazard, because its seeds are also toxic, and these can be ejected into a pond when the seed pods rupture.

The pond must also be in a relatively sheltered spot away from prevailing winds, and in a position where it will be pleasant to sit on summer evenings. It can be relatively close to the house so that it is visible from indoors, blending in with the surrounding garden. Another advantage of siting the pond near the home is that electrical apparatus to operate filters or fountains, can be connected up without too much difficulty.

On a practical basis as well, it is important that the site chosen is relatively accessible for construction purposes and is not right next to a neighbouring fence, for example. A piece of damp,

Choose a site which can be extended later if you wish.

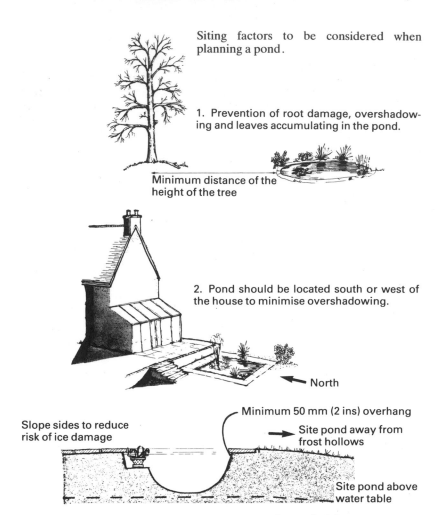

Siting factors to be considered when planning a pond.

1. Prevention of root damage, overshadowing and leaves accumulating in the pond.

Minimum distance of the height of the tree

2. Pond should be located south or west of the house to minimise overshadowing.

North

Slope sides to reduce risk of ice damage

Minimum 50 mm (2 ins) overhang

Site pond away from frost hollows

Site pond above water table

3. Consideration of frost hollows and the underlying water table.

marsky ground does not make an ideal environment for building a pond. Apart from the problems of excavation, the construction process will be made very difficult. Concrete, for example, will not dry out properly, while pool liners are liable to be forced upwards if water accumulates beneath them.

Ponds, and water gardening generally, can prove an infectious hobby, and so as a final consideration before deciding on a site, it is worth considering the possibilities for expansion at a later date. One pool, for example, may subsequently be joined to another by a waterfall, or a bog garden might later be included. Certain sites obviously allow more scope for developments of this kind.

Size

It is important to build a relatively large pond at the outset, since small areas of water prove much less satisfactory in the long term, particularly if fish are to be included. The depth is also crucial, especially in relation to the surface area of the water. In the case of a shallow pond, the water is liable to undergo greater temperature fluctuations, and apart from heating the water, sunlight will also lead to excessive algal growth under such conditions.

The pond should therefore have relatively steep sides, with a submerged shelf around its perimeter, and a deeper area of water in the centre. Its minimum area ought to be not less than 4.65 square metres (50 square feet), with the sides having a slight slope of about 1 in 3. The shelf should be about 22.5 cm (9 ins) below the final water level, while the pond should be at least 90 cm (3 feet) in depth. It will be necessary to allow approximately 45 litres per 900 square centimetres (9 to 10 gallons per square foot) of water surface. A pond which meets these criteria will allow most types of fish to be overwintered safely, while water-lilies and marginal plants can both be easily included.

Design

The actual design of the pool is largely a matter of personal preference, since it is possible to construct ponds of virtually any shape, working with certain materials. Other materials, such as fibreglass shells, obviously impose restraints, so the design of your pond is the first thing to consider before choosing your method of construction.

Ponds are often categorised on the basis of their outlines. Those with geometrical outlines, in the form of a circle or rectangle, for example, are described as formal, whereas pools designed with irregular borders are classed as informal. Those in the latter group have a more natural appearance, so that fountains and similar embellishments are usually confined to formal settings.

As a first step, a sketch of the proposed pond in relation to the rest of the garden should be drawn up. This does not need to be an elaborate plan, but it helps to give an indication of how the design will fit in to its site. Then before starting work, the proposed perimeter of the pond can be etched roughly on the ground using a trail of sand. The chosen site can then be viewed from various positions, including rooms which will ultimately overlook the pond. Any changes can be made without difficulty at this stage.

Construction

Many ponds are constructed during the early spring, when there is a spell of fine weather. They can then be stocked and planted almost immediately, so creating a good show for the summer. When building concrete ponds, however, it is best to carry out the work during the preceding autumn, but before the risk of frost which is likely to damage the structure. As explained later, these pools must be left empty for a period of time before stocking, and so if constructed in the autumn, they too will be ready for use in the spring. It may also be preferable to acquire fibreglass pools in the late summer, as many dealers sell off their surplus, often as low as half the normal price, rather than keeping them over the winter. They can be simply stored outside, base upwards, for use in the following year.

The materials and equipment needed to build and prepare a pond can be acquired from builders' merchants, larger garden centres and aquarist shops. There are also specialist water nurseries supplying the complete range of accessories, as well as plants and fish. They often advertise in fish-keeping journals, and may operate a mail-order service for customers.

Pond liners can create a natural appearance in a relatively small area.

In the case of a large pond, in particular, the hire of a small excavator may be worthwhile to carry out the bulk of the work. It is important to decide in advance where the soil will be deposited as it is removed. The top layer ought to be kept separate, since this can be re-used as a planting medium around the pond once the work is completed. The subsoil is of little value for this purpose, but can be used to good effect for creating the basis of a rock garden nearby.

Types of pond

Pond liners

As their name suggests, these are sheets of material which are simply placed in the hollow to retain the water. Polythene was first used for this purpose, but does not prove very satisfactory. Apart from being relatively easy to puncture, it is rapidly attacked by the ultraviolet rays in sunlight, and will disintegrate above the water line as a result. Polythene can be useful, however, on a temporary basis, especially if another pond has to be repaired unexpectedly. Black 500 gauge polythene proves most durable for ponds, especially if a double layer is used. Under normal conditions, it should last about a year.

Research into various materials which could be utilised as pond liners has subsequently led to the introduction of both PVC, often laminated with nylon, and butyl rubber. PVC liners are cheaper, but whereas they should remain water-tight for over a decade, butyl rubber is thought to last for perhaps fifty years. The reinforcement of PVC, with nylon or terylene, will help to increase its strength.

Butyl liners, made of a synthetic rubber which should be .075 cm (0.03 ins) in thickness, may not appear very attractive at first sight, being blackish in colour, but they create a good effect once in place. PVC liners, with a choice of blue or brown sides may seem more natural, but the darker sides of the butyl liner reflect more light, and convey a better impression of depth. Butyl rubber can be cut and fixed together using a special glue, tape or electric welding to ensure a water-tight seal.

These liners are quite easy to install, simply fitting to the contours of the hole where the pond is to be built. They are also sufficiently flexible to absorb the stresses resulting from earth movement and freezing conditions without tearing. If PVC or butyl liners are pierced accidentally, they can be repaired quite easily, in contrast to concrete ponds.

To calculate the size of liner to fit a particular pond, it is necessary to know the maximum dimensions for width, length and depth. The next step is to double the depth figure, and add

13

Calculating the size of liner required

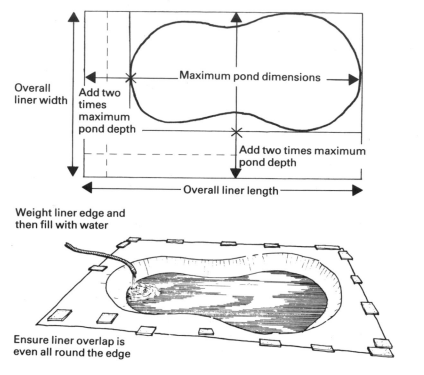

Overall liner width

Add two times maximum pond depth

Maximum pond dimensions

Add two times maximum pond depth

Overall liner length

Weight liner edge and then fill with water

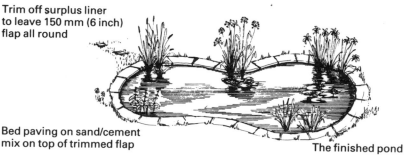

Ensure liner overlap is even all round the edge

Trim off surplus liner to leave 150 mm (6 inch) flap all round

Bed paving on sand/cement mix on top of trimmed flap

The finished pond

Stages in construction of a liner pond

this to both the width and length measurements, which will give the overall size of the liner required. With liners other than polythene, it is not necessary to allow for any additional overlap for the edges to anchor the liner around the perimeter of the pond. The flexible nature of the materials, coupled with the slope of the sides, ensures that there will be adequate available. If polythene is used, however, an extra 30 cm (12 ins) ought to be allowed for this purpose.

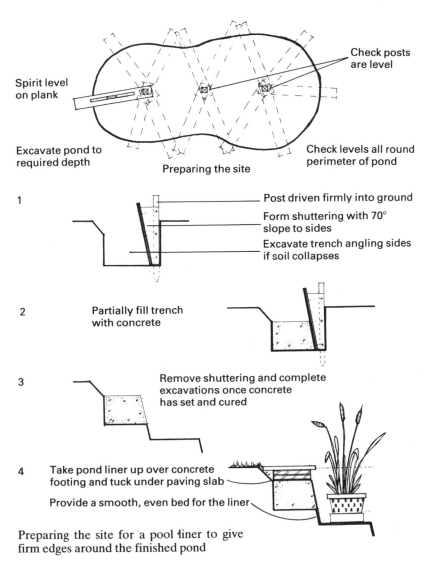

Spirit level on plank

Check posts are level

Excavate pond to required depth

Check levels all round perimeter of pond

Preparing the site

1. Post driven firmly into ground
   Form shuttering with 70° slope to sides
   Excavate trench angling sides if soil collapses

2. Partially fill trench with concrete

3. Remove shuttering and complete excavations once concrete has set and cured

4. Take pond liner up over concrete footing and tuck under paving slab
   Provide a smooth, even bed for the liner

Preparing the site for a pool liner to give firm edges around the finished pond

When excavating for a liner pond, an overall allowance of approximately 5 cm (2 ins) must be made, since the hollow will need to be covered with a thick layer of old newspapers or soft sand before the liner itself is put in place. The site should be carefully marked out, using string attached to posts, before any digging is undertaken. It is especially important to excavate the hollow with care, because the form of the liner pool will be directly dependent on the contours of the hollow. Having finished digging, it is important to remove any sharp stones or buried pieces of glass which could otherwise damage the liner, before covering the sides.

The liner can then be fitted into the hollow, checking as far as possible that there is an even overlap around the pool's perimeter. It should be roughly held in position here by bricks or paving stones at this stage. The weight of the water will ensure that the liner fits snugly to the hollow, and the pond can be filled easily using a hose. As the pond fills, the water stretches the liner, firming it back against the sides of the hollow and any shelving.

Although it may be necessary to remove some of the supporting weight, enough tension must be maintained on the liner at this stage to prevent it creasing excessively. Any creases which do become apparent can be minimised by cautious manipulation of the liner while the pond is filling. Polythene liners will need to be smoothed into place before the water is added, since they are relatively inelastic.

Ready-made pools

At first sight, the idea of a pre-formed shell which simply fits into a hole in the ground and then has to be filled with water seems the most convenient option for a garden pond. In reality though, the majority of these moulded pools leave much to be desired in terms of their design. While they are available in a range of different shapes to suit most sites, the majority are too small, or not deep enough to be adequate for overwintering fish successfully.

These ponds are generally made out of either fibreglass or plastic. Those made of plastic are invariably cheaper, but are also more easily damaged. Although not difficult to site, it is very important to check, as with all ponds, by using a spirit level, that the preformed shell is level in the ground before it is filled. This type of pond can be useful for breeding quarters for a particular pair of fish, and also for quarantine purposes. In view of their depth, they are well-suited to the needs of children, making an ideal hatching environment for frog and toad spawn, for example. Unfortunately, the sides of such ponds are too smooth to allow terrapins to climb out of the water and sun themselves. Otherwise they would adapt well for this purpose during the summer months.

It is not, in fact, essential to bury these ponds in the ground. Debris such as leaves will then collect around the base of the structure, rather than actually polluting the water itself. The unattractive sides can be disguised with stone work or similar material. Moulded ponds are relatively easy to clean out, as they can be removed from their site once empty, and hosed down thoroughly to remove the silt which will have accumulated in the bottom.

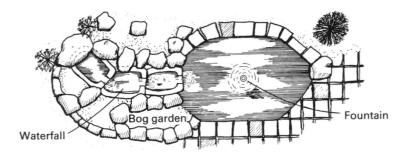

Plan of pond with waterfall, constructed of preformed sections

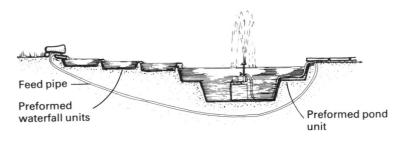

Feed pipe

Preformed waterfall units

Preformed pond unit

Section through pond and waterfall

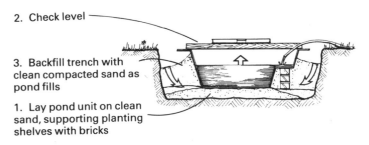

2. Check level

3. Backfill trench with clean compacted sand as pond fills

1. Lay pond unit on clean sand, supporting planting shelves with bricks

Siting a fibreglass pond

Concrete ponds

Concrete is the traditional material for building a pond, but has been superceded to a large extent by the previous methods. Building a concrete pond is a relatively laborious and quite expensive task. It is, however, a reliable, flexible method, being suitable for any given shape or depth, providing construction is carried out with care. Concrete ponds are very durable, and cannot be punctured. Yet concrete will fracture spontaneously if incorrectly laid and such leaks are difficult to seal.

Shuttering is required to act as a mould for the wet concrete, holding it against the sides of the excavation. Wood is normally used for this purpose, but plywood is a useful alternative, providing it does not collapse under the weight of the wet concrete, if a curved outline is required. Hardboard may not be strong enough.

Construction of a concrete pond normally starts with its base. Once the site is excavated, hardcore to a depth of 15 cm (6 ins) must be tightly packed into the floor. Old bricks and similar materials are ideal, and should be pounded into place to minimise the potential effects of any later subsidence.

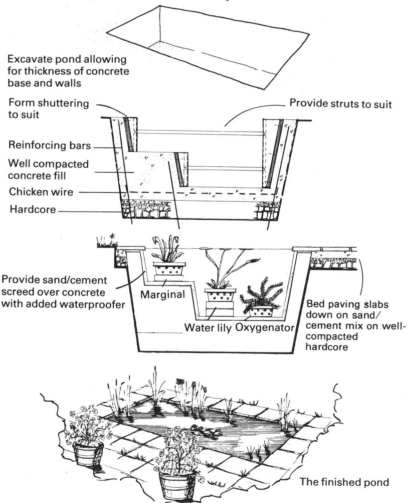

Excavate pond allowing for thickness of concrete base and walls

Form shuttering to suit

Provide struts to suit

Reinforcing bars

Well compacted concrete fill

Chicken wire

Hardcore

Provide sand/cement screed over concrete with added waterproofer

Marginal

Water lily Oxygenator

Bed paving slabs down on sand/cement mix on well-compacted hardcore

The finished pond

Formal concrete pond — construction stages

Mixing large amounts of concrete is hard work, and it may be worth hiring a small concrete mixer. In any event, the concrete should be prepared as close to the site as possible so that it will not have to be transported large distances. Without a mixer, a large piece of hardboard can act as a mixing board. Using a bucket as the standard measure, the concrete should consist of one part of cement to two parts of sharp sand and three parts of coarse ballast. These ingredients must then be mixed thoroughly together with a spade before any water is actually added. This helps to ensure a better final result and makes easier work of the mixing, since the dry ingredients are much lighter to turn.

Once the mix is of an even colour, make a depression in the centre, and add the water. Only a relatively small amount of water must be introduced at one time, with the concrete being stirred thoroughly in between so that it does not become too sloppy. A fairly stiff mixture is required, particularly for the walls, so that it will remain in place without sliding down the sides of the excavation.

The base is laid first, to a depth of about 12.5 cm (5 ins), by simply shovelling the concrete on top of the hardcore and spreading it roughly over the site. The depth can be measured using a pencil as a probe, and holding this against a ruler. It is worth doing this in several places to ensure an even covering.

Once the base is relatively dry, shuttering should be fitted as necessary, held in place by stakes driven into the ground. As the concrete is introduced behind the shuttering, it must be smeared against the earth walls, using a spade or trowel. There is no need to ensure a smooth finish at this stage, but dipping the trowel into a bucket of water between applications of concrete should help to prevent it sticking to the tool. All equipment must, of course, be washed off thoroughly immediately after use to prevent concrete setting hard on it.

In the first instance, the outline of the pond should only be covered to a depth of 7.5 cm (3 ins). The next day, another layer must be applied to give an overall thickness of 15 cm (6 ins).It is useful, especially with a large pond, to strengthen the base and sides using chicken wire set into the concrete, taking care to ensure that no loose ends protrude through into the pool itself.

The final coat of concrete, which will need to applied over the whole surface, adding an extra 2.5 cm (1 inch) to the thickness, is made differently, using one part of cement to three parts of sharp sand, prepared as before. A water-proofing powder must also be added to the mixture, as directed on the packet.

It is vital that this layer is applied in one session, and smoothed off carefully to eliminate any air bubbles which may be present in the wet concrete. The pond should then be left to dry out thoroughly, although not too rapidly. In hot weather, the concrete will need to be protected under damp sacking to prevent the sun drying it out too quickly, which will lead to a soft, flaky surface. Leave the pond for at least a week before the water is introduced.

The concrete at this stage will contain large amounts of lime, which must be allowed to come out into solution, so it can be removed before fish and plants are added. Although it is possible to treat the surface of the concrete with chemicals to retain the lime in the concrete, this can be hazardous. If any of the seal over the concrete is lost, the lime will then dissolve into the water, poisoning all pond life in the process.

Repeated filling and emptying of the pond is therefore the safest method of dissipating the lime. Water should be left in the pond for a week, and then its sides must be thoroughly scrubbed with a stiff brush before the water is emptied. This procedure will have to be repeated for about two months, monitoring progress by means of pH tests. Once the reading on the test strip is safe, the pond can be drained for a final time before being refilled and made ready for its inhabitants.

Block ponds

An alternative to the concrete pond is a structure built using either bricks or cement blocks. This method is especially useful for raised ponds. The base is prepared as before, with the blocks being left to soak in water. Then once the base is ready, the blocks are put in place, as if building ordinary walls. Overlapping of the blocks on top of each other to give structural stability is obviously essential, as is the use of a spirit level to ensure a level structure.

After the perimeter walls have set in position, the rendering as described previously must be applied all round the inner surfaces of the pond, wetting the blocks beforehand to ensure this layer attaches well. The outer face of the walls can either be pointed, rendered or covered with stone as desired. It is then a matter of once again allowing the lime to come out into solution, before the pond can be used.

Raised ponds of this type are less tedious to construct than their concrete counterparts, and there is no problem to be faced over disposing of the large amounts of earth which would otherwise have to be excavated. The occupants of a raised pond are often easier to spot, and there is much less risk of falling into them. They are ideal for both young and old alike. The surrounds of such a pool can be developed to form an attractive rock garden.

Clay ponds

Clay used to be an important material for pond construction.

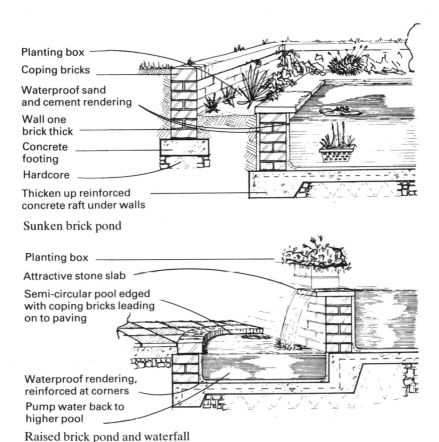

Planting box
Coping bricks
Waterproof sand and cement rendering
Wall one brick thick
Concrete footing
Hardcore
Thicken up reinforced concrete raft under walls

Sunken brick pond

Planting box
Attractive stone slab
Semi-circular pool edged with coping bricks leading on to paving
Waterproof rendering, reinforced at corners
Pump water back to higher pool

Raised brick pond and waterfall

The Dewponds, across the South Downs of England, were built on porous chalk, by means of an impermeable clay base. They provided an important reservoir of water for the sheep which grazed on the downland, and although changes in agriculture have made them largely redundant, many can still be seen today. Puddled clay ponds of this type require a layer of clay about 30 cm (1 foot) in thickness. The clay has to be worked to a consistency of plasticine before being smeared all over the hollow. The results of this work in amateur hands are not always reliable, but with a ready source of clay it is the cheapest means of pond construction.

Modern developments

The introduction of black polyester pools to the British market for the 1983 season appears to represent a significant improvement in the moulded pool market. This material, which is used for boat construction, is extremely strong, and the ponds themselves are guaranteed for ten years. Some of the designs are large enough for koi carp, which require more space than other fish.

Equipping and finishing the pond

Filters

Many ponds do not include a filtration system of any kind, but unless the pond is to be very lightly stocked with fish, some means of filtering the water to remove the waste products which accumulate is recommended. If koi are to be kept, a filter is an essential piece of equipment, as these fish are susceptible to the changes in the water chemistry which will otherwise occur. There is also likely to be more algal contamination in koi ponds, since in the absence of plants, these organisms flourish on the resulting high level of nitrates present in the water.

Filters for ponds operate on the same principles as those used in aquaria. Mechanical filtration is the simplest method, involving the removal of solid particles of debris by means of a suitable medium which retains them. In any pond, biological filtration occurs naturally, with bacteria present in the water breaking down organic waste matter to beneficial nitrate, which can then be utilised by the plants for their growth. Chemical filtration entails the use of a compound to act upon the debris, and effectively neutralise it.

Pond filters are generally divided into one of two categories. Undergravel filters are normally incorporated into the design of the pond itself, and therefore are relatively unobtrusive, although the pond will have to be made considerably deeper to accommodate a filter of this type. Filtration is achieved by biological means and so the air pump attached to the filter will have to be left on continuously in order to ensure an adequate supply of oxygen for the bacteria which will degrade the waste matter. With a filter of this type, no chemical treatments should be added to the water, since they are likely to destroy these beneficial bacteria and thus compromise the filtration system.

Undergravel filters must cover an area equivalent to at least a third of the pond's surface. They are constructed using rigid

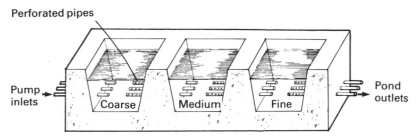

Perforated pipes

Pump inlets →

Pond outlets

Coarse   Medium   Fine

Multi-compartment external filter, using different grades of filter media

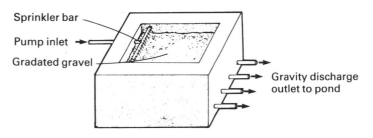

Sprinkler bar

Pump inlet →

Gradated gravel

Gravity discharge outlet to pond

Simple box external filter

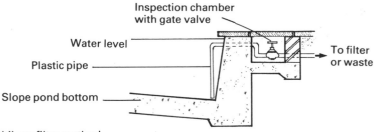

Inspection chamber with gate valve

Water level

Plastic pipe

Slope pond bottom

To filter or waste

Koshihara filter method

Types of filter

plastic tubing, which needs to be 1.9-2.5 cm (¾-1 inch) in diameter, to ensure an adequate air flow. Within the external frame, additional pipes spaced about 20 cm (8 ins) apart must be connected to the framework by means of T-pieces. Corners are made using curved junctions. An outer exit must be left to be joined up to the air pump itself once the filter is fitted in the pond. To enable the air to escape, all straight lengths of tubing must be drilled, using a bit of 6 mm (³⁄₁₆-¼ inch) diameter. The holes themselves should be spaced about 2.5 cm (1 inch) apart, being slightly closer when on the furthest side from the pump. This is most easily done by holding the tubing with clamps or in a vice.

The filter will have to be buried under a layer of at least 30 cm (1 foot), preferably 45 cm (18 ins) of gravel. A relatively coarse grade, with particles of 1.9 cm (¾ inch) is best, since this will not clog up rapidly. Although such gravel is sold already washed, it is generally quite dirty, and will benefit from further washing. It may also harbour disease, and ought to be treated to overcome this risk.

It should first be tipped into an inflated pool containing salt water, made up using 6 g of salt per litre of water (1 oz to 1 gallon), and left to soak overnight. Small amounts can then be removed in a colander and rinsed off under a tap. Although tedious, this method will ensure that there is no scum on the top of the pond resulting from dirty gravel.

Depending on the design of the base of the pond, the filter can be positioned in a relatively shallow part where it will be accessible, allowing the fish to escape to deeper water if it has to be taken up. Such filters should not require any maintenance, however, and so are best sited in the deepest water, where all the debris can accumulate above it.

An external filter does not actually fit in the pond. Water is drawn off by the pump, passes through the filter and then returns to the pond. A basic external filter is made up of a trough built of bricks covered in water-proof paint. The inlet piping is set at a relatively high level, while the outlet, on the opposite side, is positioned at the base of the trough. This must be of a wider bore to minimise the risk of flooding. An overflow can also be included at a point level with the inlet, as an additional precaution.

Pea gravel, prepared as before, is generally used to fill the trough up to a level just below the inlet pipes. It is possible to construct a sequence of such filters, with water flowing from one filter bed into the next, through progressively smaller gravel, so that finer particles are removed at each stage. Silver sand can be used in the last trough before the water is returned to the pond. This will help to filter out algae, and so reduces the problem of green water, which is not only unsightly, but can lower the oxygen content of the water itself. The flow must always be in the direction of progressively less coarse filter media and never the reverse, since this will rapidly cause a blockage of the filter material, leading to an overflow.

External filters can be disguised to good effect, using them to form the base of a seat. As an alternative, they can be sunk into the ground, although in this case, the inlet and outlet heights will have to be reversed, so that the water enters at a lower level than it leaves, facilitating its return to the pond.

Barrel filters are of the external type, but have a more simple design. No inlet is required, since the water is introduced by means of a sprinkler from above, directly on to the gravel. It is important, however, to ensure that the head of the sprinkler does not become blocked with debris, thus reducing its efficiency.

As an alternative to gravel, some filters are filled with clinker, while commercial models rely on other materials such as special small porcelain balls. These fulfil an identical function though, and need to be tipped evenly over the base of the filter, up to the required height. Several manufacturers have also introduced effective filters of various types which fit in the pond itself, and the majority are quite straightforward to service when necessary.

Pumps

The effectiveness of the filtration system will be influenced by the working of the pump. In the case of an undergravel filter, the pump will be required to draw a quarter of the total volume of water through each hour. A relatively powerful pump will prove the best investment. As well as supplying the filter, pumps also circulate water through fountains and waterfalls. They can be divided into two categories.

Submersible pumps, as their name suggests, are located beneath the water's surface. The whole unit is enclosed in a water-proof casing which protects the electric motor, with the impeller actually driving the water through the pump. Submersible pumps are very easy to install, since they only need to be connected to a mains supply, although the power supply can be routed via a transformer, which is a safer option. A gauze fits over the inlet so that plants and fish cannot be drawn into the pump with the water. An adjuster on the outer casing will ensure that the flow rate can be regulated as needed. This feature is especially important for pumps supplying fountains.

Surface or external pumps are useful for large ponds, since they have a larger capacity, but are also more expensive than submersibles. They need to be housed out of the water, yet close to the pond. Water is circulated via piping with a strainer at the end, and then passed by another tube from the pump. This allows considerable flexibility, since by means of stop cocks on the outlet pipe it is possible to supply water to both a fountain and a waterfall simultaneously. These can then be shut off, while a third stop cock gives provision for emptying the pond.

The pump house itself must be designed to give adequate space so that the parts are easily accessible. It needs to be built to minimise the risk of flooding, with drainage holes included in the base. A water-tight lid is also essential. A stop cock should also be included on the inlet pipe, in order to prevent water being sucked into the pump when it is not in operation.

Siphon filters

While both undergravel and external filters have to be powered by means of a pump, the Koshihara system works on the siphon principle. It is popular for use in ponds containing koi, although the pool will need to be designed in advance to accommodate this filter. The bottom of the pond must slope so that a corner will be the deepest point once it is filled. A plastic pipe is fitted vertically directly above this area and quite close to the bottom. It then leaves from the pond by means of a corner junction giving a 90° turn just below the water level, before dipping down again, and connecting to a stop cock.

In order to ensure an effective flow of water when the valve is opened, the outlet must be positioned below the surface water level of the pond. It is also necessary to set the system in operation once the pipework is in place, by using a hose to force all the air out of the tubing into the pond. When no bubbles come to the surface, the stop cock should be closed. Flow of water will then start whenever the valve is turned, providing no air enters the system as will happen if the pond is emptied completely. Suction of the water through the piping will also draw the debris which will have accumulated below the pipe at the lowest level in the pond. Fresh dechlorinated water of the correct temperature is then added to the pond to replace the volume which was drained off. This can be used to good effect on flower beds, since it contains dissolved nitrates, and thus acts as a fertiliser.

Fountains

Many designs of fountain are available, and apart from differing in shape, they also have jets of various types, creating different patterns of cascades. Most people like to have a good sized water spout. The height of the jet is a variable feature, however, which depends on an individual pump's capacity and the actual throughput of water. By restricting the flow, less water will be ejected, but since it is under greater pressure, the fountain will reach a greater height. The circulation of water via a fountain is of benefit to fish, but the spray must be directed away from plants as much as possible.

The head of the fountain should be located above the water level, and thus when used in conjunction with a submersible pump, a secure base for the combination will be required. If rockwork is necessary for this purpose, only insoluble stones such as granite and quartz should be included, because limestone rocks will dissolve in the water and may well poison the fish. Alternatively, a plastic water-tight container filled with

Ornamental fountain

Submersible pump suitable for waterfalls

Pump for waterfall with fountain set to suit

'Otter mini' pump, suitable for
smaller heads of water

Pumps and fountains

sand or rocks can be used for the purpose, and is likely to give a firmer base.

A problem likely to be encountered in small ponds with a high fountain spout is that the spray is liable to fall outside the area of water surface. Any loss of water will need to be made up, using a dechlorinated supply only. Chemicals which can be added to tap water for this purpose are widely available from most aquarist dealers, and avoid the need to leave water standing for several days to allow the gas to come out of solution. Loss of water can be reduced by positioning the fountain centrally in the largest area of water, and by adjusting the height of the spout on windy days. This is more conveniently done by means of an external pump, since the alteration can be carried out without having to reach the pump in the deepest part of the pond.

Pond ornaments

Ornaments, such as cherubs or fish which also act as fountains, must be connected to pumps in a slightly different manner. A piece of tubing links the pump to the ornament, with clips used on either end of the piping to keep it in place. In this case, it will not be necessary to site a submersible pump operating the water spout in the centre of the pond, so that its height can be more easily adjusted.

Care must be taken with such ornaments to ensure that they will not release lime into the water, as the majority are made of concrete rather than an inert material like plastic. The cost of such ornaments varies considerably, depending on the materials used in construction. Cast ornaments made of bronze or lead have a very long life span but are correspondingly expensive, whereas cheaper plaster figures used for decoration around the pond are not very durable out of doors.

The range of ornaments produced is wide and varied, and although not to everyone's taste, they are nevertheless popular. They include ducks and frogs which can be sited in the shallows, the traditional garden gnome complete with fishing rod, and even complete sets, such as representations of Snow White and the Seven Dwarfs.

Rather than buying the ornaments themselves, it is possible to obtain moulds. These are made of rubber and can be used repeatedly. They are stocked by many hobby shops, or can be acquired by mail order, direct from suppliers. The first step is to bury the mould bottom up in a bed of sawdust or sand. A mixture of one part of sharp sand to one part of cement will be used to form the case, and must be mixed as described under building a concrete pond (page 19) to achieve a thick yet relatively fluid consistency.

As the concrete is introduced to the mould, it is vital to rock the mould back and forth to force air bubbles out before they can set in place and weaken the resulting cast. Once the concrete has become firm, the ornament is removed by thoroughly soaping the outside of the mould, and peeling it back on itself. The casts can be painted if desired, after being left to harden completely in the air, and may also be glazed.

Lighting

Pond lighting can be used to good effect to emphasise particular features of the pond, and need not be intrusive if sited carefully. Floating lights are available and these are especially useful for highlighting fountains. They operate through a 12 volt transformer, and may also be adapted for submersion by attaching a

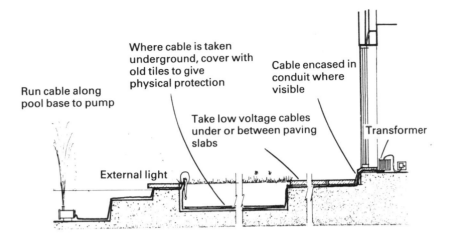

Where cable is taken underground, cover with old tiles to give physical protection

Cable encased in conduit where visible

Run cable along pool base to pump

Take low voltage cables under or between paving slabs

Transformer

External light

Providing an electrical supply to pump and lights

suitable weight to each light. Only those which state clearly they can be used in this way should be placed in the water. Other 12 volt systems can be acquired to illuminate the surrounds of the pond.

Sets of such lights are available attached to the necessary cable and the transformer. It is worth checking on the availability of replacement bulbs. Changing bulbs in totally sealed units is difficult, whereas those lights which simply use car light bulbs can easily be opened so that the bulb can be changed, taking care that the outer cap is replaced properly afterwards. Some manufacturers produce filter lights, so that the actual colour can be changed simply by altering the lens at the front.

Floodlights running direct off mains voltage are also available and give off much greater light. Again, a range of colours can be obtained, the choice depending on the effect which is to be created. Green shrubs for example, will be highlighted by use of a green light. It is important to position floodlights in such a way that they will not blind the onlooker, or a neighbour.

Safety

Great care must be taken when using electricity in close proximity to water. Safety is obviously of paramount importance to the manufacturers of such items, but it is up to the operator to ensure that they are used correctly, and the mains supply is located in a water-proof position. A particular source of danger can result from having to join cables. The majority of pumps and lights have adequate flex to avoid this. If in any doubt about the electrical set-up, then advice from a professional electrician should be sought. In addition, it is important not to disguise the cable, or leave it in a position where it could be cut, for example by a lawn mower at a later date.

Finishing the surrounds

The area around the pond should be paved, irrespective of the material which has been used for construction. While grass edging may appear more attractive at first, especially around an informal pond, it will deteriorate rapidly into muddy patches, which may in turn be colonised by moss.

Pond liners should be trimmed back if necessary around the edge; the surplus can be kept for patching a leak at a later date. It is usual when laying the paving to overlap about 2.5 cm (1 inch) over the pond itself. This will help to protect the liner from direct sunlight, where it is above the water-level.

A path may also be needed to connect the pond to an existing walkway. This route should be planned out, using string, before any turf is cut away. The paving stones must be laid level, and sufficient soil will need to be removed so that they can be set on a base of gravel or clinker level with the surrounding turf. The type of paving used depends partly on the pond itself. Regular concrete slabs are usually laid around a formal pool, whereas York stone or a similar material may be preferred to create crazy paving in more informal surroundings.

There are various plants which can be grown in and around the path. Those with scented foliage are popular since their perfume becomes especially evident when they are trodden underfoot. Certain low-growing thymes and mints are ideal. A small annual, *Ionopsidium acaule* is another alternative. When planted thinly in spring around the paving, it will soon produce a mass of mauvish flowers. *Ionopsidium* is a small plant, only growing to a height of about 1.25 cm (½ inch).

Rock gardens

Faced with the mass of soil from the excavation for the pond, it may be possible to utilise this as the basis for an attractive rock garden. Careful planning must be undertaken though, to ensure the best possible effect is created, including provision for the construction of a stream or waterfall linking up with the pond at a later date.

The site for the rock garden must be well-drained. In the case of heavy clay soils, it may be necessary to actually dig another hole, in the centre of the proposed site, and fill this with gravel or clinker, so that water can drain away quickly. Water-logging of the soil will rapidly kill the plants. A site which has both shady and sunny aspects is best, so that a wide range of plants can be included; a south-facing location being generally preferable.

The upper few centimetres of soil are most fertile, and ideally this should have been dug off first and kept in a separate heap when excavating the pond. It can then be used to form the top layer of the rock garden. If required, it is possible to purchase additional 'top soil' for this purpose. Alternatively, a combination of moss peat, sharp sand and fibrous loam, mixed to a ratio of 2:1½:4, using a bucket as the standard measure, will be suitable.

There are various types of stone available, although the high transport costs mean that it is usually best to buy local stone. In southern England for example, Sussex sandstone is commonly used in the construction of rock gardens. The west Sussex stone is reddish, whereas that from the east of the county is greyish, and quarried in more regular shapes. It is worth visiting a stone merchant to see the type and colour of stone available in a particular area.

A huge range of plants can be included in the rock garden, although certain species will spread very rapidly and may take over large areas unless their growth is severely curtailed. Another consideration must be to select plants with a view to providing colour throughout the year, and not just in the summer. Alyssum and yellow aubretia are very attractive and will grow profusely, yet only flower in the spring. Growing conditions will also influence the choice of plants. Asian gentians for example, flowering late in the year, require a chalk-free soil, whereas *Houstonia caerulea* likes a shady spot and will produce bright blue flowers during the early summer.

Landscaping with aquatic plants

Plants in the pond itself are obviously attractive, but also have other important functions in maintaining an overall balance within the environment. They utilise waste products of fish, once these have been broken down by bacteria, and also provide hiding and spawning sites. Broad-leaved plants, by spreading over the water's surface, decrease the amount of sunlight actually penetrating into the pond, and so reduce the growth of algae, which will otherwise turn the water green.

The various plants used in the setting of a water garden are broadly classified into one of four groups. Marginal plants, as their name suggests, are cultivated in shallow water around the edge of the pond. They are a diverse group of plants, in contrast to the instantly recognisable water-lilies, which form another category. These plants are available in a wide range of colours, and need a relatively large area and adequate depth of water, depending on the variety concerned.

Floating plants do not root in the traditional sense, but live on the surface of the water. While individually often small, this group can spread rapidly, taking over the pond in the process. Oxygenating plants are particularly important for fish, being used for spawning grounds, although their role as oxygen-producers is of relatively small significance. They are confined to the body of the water itself.

Marginal plants

The following selection, listed alphabetically, includes the most popular and hardy varieties suitable for all types of pond.

Acorus calamus variegatus   This is the more colourful form of Sweet Flag, which grows wild in certain parts of Norfolk. Its yellow and green striped leaves resemble those of an iris in shape. If crushed, they give off a characteristic odour. The flower itself is relatively inconspicuous, being cone-shaped and greenish-brown in colour. The rhizome must be planted in a few centimetres of water only, with the resulting plant growing to a height of 90 cm (3 feet) or so.

Two other forms of *Acorus* are occasionally encountered. *A. gramineus* is smaller, reaching a size of 25 cm (10 ins), with finer leaves and lacking the colour of *A. c. variegatus*. Another Japanese species, *A. g. pusillus* grows even shorter, and should be confined to very shallow water.

Aponogeton distachyos   Popularly known as the Water Hawthorn, this plant produces white flowers with black centres in the shape of a 'V'. It has a sweet scent, and blooms throughout the summer. The leaves have an unusual elongated oval form. Pink and reddish varieties of *Aponogeton* are also available. These plants are quite adaptable, growing in deeper water than many other marginals, up to a depth of about 60 cm (2 feet). Division of root stock is the easiest means of propagation, but *Aponogeton* can be grown from seed as well. It is a rapid grower when planted in the spring.

Acorus calamus

Aponogeton distachyos

33

***Butomus umbellatus* (Flowering Rush; Water Gladiolus)** A marginal which is attractive throughout much of the growing season. Its sword-shaped leaves are purplish at first, turning green as they mature. The flowers are not similar to gladioli in shape, however, but grow in clusters off a central stem and are rose-pink in colour. The Flowering Rush can reach a size of about 90 cm (3 feet).

***Calla palustris* (Bog Arum)** This plant, with its heart-shaped leaves, requires relatively shallow water, and will grow to about 15 cm (6 ins) in height. Clusters of Bog Arum create the best effect, although the fragrant white flowers may not develop in the first year. The red berries which follow the blooms will be attractive during the autumn.

***Caltha* species (Marsh Marigolds)** These are amongst the earliest of the marginal plants to flower, and are particularly colourful in the early spring. Various forms are available. The Common Marsh Marigold (*C. palustris*) has blooms resembling those of a buttercup, growing between 22.5 and 37.5 cm (9 and 15 ins) in height. It will do well in either wet surroundings or shallow water. A more elaborate form is *C. p. plena*, which has double flowers. The largest species is *C. polypetala*, which can grow to a height of 90 cm (3 feet), having flowers 7.5 cm (3 ins) in diameter. As with other members of the genus, its roots should be confined, by means of a suitable container, to restrict its spread around the pond.

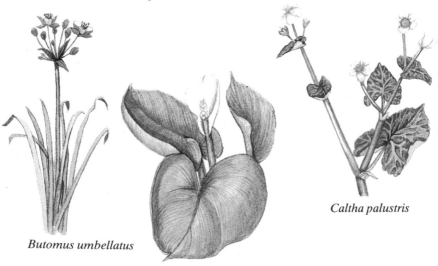

Caltha palustris

Butomus umbellatus

Calla palustris

Iris **species**   The Iris is a popular marginal plant, by virtue of its striking leaves and colourful flowers, and a wide range of these plants are now cultivated. *I. laevigata* will do well if planted under several centimetres of water. It reaches a size of about 60 cm (2 feet), and has thin leaves, offset against deep blue flowers which have a contrasting white region down the centres of the outer petals. Other forms of this iris include Snowdrift, with snowy-white flowers and *albopurpurea* which is violet-blue.

One of the best-known irises is *I. pseudocorus*, known as the Yellow Flag, and also the 'Fleur-de-Lys' of France. It has bright yellow flowers and grows to a height of about 90 cm (3 feet). These plants show to best effect when planted in small groups, although they are also popular as cut flowers. *I. sibirica* is often cultivated for this purpose, producing bluish blooms. It does best in very damp soil, rather than being actually underwater, and so should be planted in a relatively tall container for the marginal shelf of the pond, producing its blooms during May and June. Irises with variegated leaves such as *I. kaempferii variegata* are also available. In this case, the leaves are green and cream, while the flowers are rich purple.

Iris pseudacorus   *Mimulus guttatus*

Mimulus **(Musk)**   This is a colourful group of marginals, although they are not hardy. Some, such as *M. cardinalis*, can be grown from seed. This variety has scarlet and yellow flowers, and reaches a height of about 45 cm (18 ins). The Monkey Musk (*M. luteus*), with yellow flowers, grows to approximately 30 cm (1 foot) in height, and does best in shallow water, less than 7.5 cm (3 ins) deep. The Lavender Musk (*M. ringens*), so called because of the colour of its flowers, is a tall species reaching a size of 60 cm (2 feet). It flowers relatively late in the year.

***Myosotis palustris* (Water Forget-me-not)**   The aquatic form is a deeper coloured blue than the common garden variety, and its flowers last longer. These plants are easily grown from seed, but should not be planted in water deeper than 7.5 cm (3 ins). A white form is also available.

***Pontederia cordata* (Pickerel Weed)**   An impressive plant, with glossy, heart-shaped leaves, which grows to about 60 cm (2 feet) high. It flowers quite late in the year, producing blue flowers on spikes, which are similar to delphiniums.

***Ranunculus lingua* (Giant Water Buttercup or Spearwort)**   This marginal grows to a maximum height of about 90 cm (3 feet), and produces bright yellow flowers. It is usually grown from seed, and will do well in water up to 15 cm (6 ins) in depth. Another *Ranunculus* species *R. aquatilis*, is commonly grown as an oxygenator, whereas others are classed as floating plants.

Pontederia cordata

Ranunculus lingua

Sagittaria sagittifolia

***Sagittaria* species (Arrowhead)**   The common name of these plants is derived from the shape of their leaves, which resembles the tip of an arrow. *S. japonica* produces attractive white double flowers. It grows to the height of about 30 cm (1 foot). The smaller form *S. sagittifolia* is ideal for the smaller pond, and also produces masses of double white flowers. Arrowheads are usually propagated by means of tubers, and need to be planted in shallow water about 12.5 cm (5 ins) deep.

***Scirpus zebrinus* (Zebra Rush)**   The Zebra Rush is valued for its foliage, which is a combination of green and white. Set to the back of the pond, this rush may grow to a size of about 90 cm (3 feet), producing a good background effect. Other similar rushes in this genus include the true Bulrush (*S. tabernaemontani*). In the case of *S. laetivirens aureus*, the striping on the leaves is more golden than white. All these rushes are propagated by dividing root stock.

***Typha* (Reed Mace)**   Members of this genus are often incorrectly described as bulrushes, but should be known as Reed Maces. The Great Reed Mace (*T. latifola*) produces the long characteristic brown seed-heads, and reaches a height of about 120 cm (4 feet). It is not suitable for most smaller ponds, however, because it grows by spreading its roots at a fast pace, rapidly dominating the pond. Two smaller species are *T. laxmanni*, which grows to 90 cm (3 feet), and the dwarf Japanese variety *T. minima*. This type produces spikes which are approximately 7.5 cm (3 ins) in length, and also flowers freely. The growth of all reed maces should be limited by planting them in suitable containers.

Scirpus tabernaemontani zebrinus

Typha minima

37

Oxygenators

A selection of oxygenating plants should be included in every pond, especially where fish are present. They will be a source of food, as well as providing breeding ground and shelter. The role in producing oxygen for the fish is perhaps the least significant of their functions. Under conditions of bright light, plants take up carbon dioxide and liberate oxygen by the process of photosynthesis. In poor light, or darkness, oxygenating plants utilise oxygen, like other plants and indeed the fish themselves.

Oxygenating plants grow rapidly, which can be advantageous, especially in a newly-established pond. They will take up nutrients through their leaves and, as water-lilies develop on the surface, algae, which would otherwise thrive and cloud the water, are deprived of both sunlight and nutrients. These plants are sold in the form of cuttings, and although they can just be allowed to float in the pond, it is preferable to root them in a particular area.

Callitriche

Ceratophyllum demersum

***Callitriche* (Water Starwort)**   This is an aquatic plant which is native to Britain, named after the star-like pattern of its pale foliage, seen from above. Two forms are recognised with *C. hermaphroditica* being especially valuable during the autumn, while *C. palustris* makes more growth in the early part of the year.

Ceratophyllum demersum   This has leaves arranged in whorls around its stems. It is brittle, with pieces often breaking off and rooting separately.

***Chara* (Stonewort)**   Rather similar to the preceding species, Stonewort has sharp foliage, with an unpleasant smell.

***Elodea* species**   Members of this genus are the most widely-used oxygenators, being freely available from the majority of aquarist stores. The Canadian Pondweed (*E. canadensis*) is a native of North America, and has a justifiable reputation for growing very rapidly, especially in a new pond. It has attractive dark green foliage. A similar related variety is *E. crispa* (*Lagarosiphon major*), which is a native of South Africa. It is nevertheless hardy enough to overwinter successfully in outdoor ponds.

***Fontinalis* (Willow Moss)**   Unlike other oxygenators, Willow Moss is often found attached to sunken rocks or wood. Its appearance resembles that of moss, and it is dark green in colour. It thrives in quite shady conditions, but does not produce any attractive flowers.

***Hottonia palustris* (Water Violet)**   The Water Violet yields mauvish flowers above the water's surface, while its attractive green leaves remain submerged. It has an interesting cycle, with buds produced later in the year falling to the bottom of the pond and re-emerging during the following spring to start up new growth. The flowers themselves may extend 25 cm (10 ins) or so into the air, and for this reason it is considered the most attractive member of this group of plants.

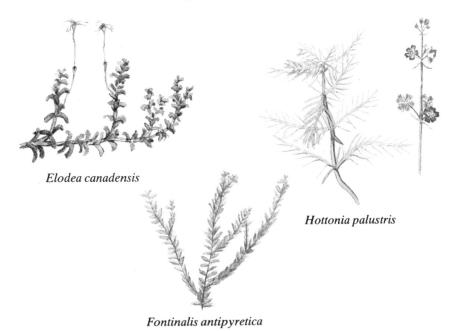

Elodea canadensis

Hottonia palustris

Fontinalis antipyretica

***Myriophyllum* (Water Milfoil)**   Characterised by its fine-leaved appearance, *Myriophyllum* resembles Hornwort, although its whorled leaf structure is relatively flat. It will not do well in ponds where there is a heavy concentration of algae or other debris which will settle on its leaves. Unfortunately the attractive reddish form, *M. rubrifolium* is not sufficiently hardy for an outdoor setting. Cuttings, as with all these plants, root readily, even when not in direct contact with a suitable substrate.

Nitella gracilis   Another species with narrow leaves, *Nitella* can grow very thickly, and thus provides an ideal retreat for fry. It also spreads quite rapidly in warm, relatively shallow water.

Potamogeton   Members of this genus are loosely described as Pondweed. The majority are confined underwater, but some do occur on the surface. Individual pieces can grow into very long strands, creating an untidy, weedy appearance. These plants are not in fact, particularly useful oxygenators. The Curled Pondweed (*P. crispus*) has wavy edges to its leaves which are about 7.5 cm (3 ins) long and 1.25 cm (½ inch) wide. These turn an attractive reddish colour in good light.

Myriophyllum spicatum

Potamogeton crispus

Proserpinaca palustris (**Mermaid Weed**) A popular oxygen-ating plant which grows wild in parts of North America. When submerged, the leaves are relatively fine, compared to those growing in the air. It flowers above the water surface, but is normally cultivated from cuttings and not seed.

Ranunculus aquatilis (**Water Crowfoot**) This plant also has two types of leaves, depending on its growing environment. Those in water are thread-like, whereas foliage floating on the surface has three distinct lobes. *R. aquatilis* produces attractive white flowers during the early part of the year, whereas a North American species, *R. delphinifolius* has yellow blooms. These plants can both spread very rapidly in the pond.

Utricularia (**Bladderwort**) An interesting group of plants which actually catch small creatures such as Daphnia in bladder-like structures on their stems. The British species, *U. vulgaris* produces yellow flowers resembling those of a snapdragon, above the water's surface.

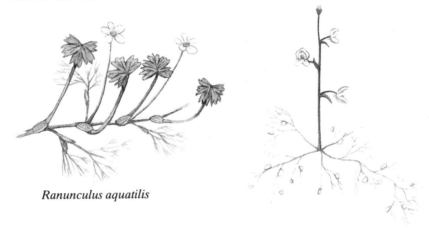

Ranunculus aquatilis

Utricularia vulgaris

Floating plants

This description is applied to a large number of plants which are able to sustain themselves at the surface of the pond without having their roots anchored. Again, they provide food, shade and shelter for fish, while their roots can be utilised as a spawning ground by some species.

Azolla caroliniana (**Fairy Moss**) This is a species which has become naturalised in Britain, although it originates from America. Like the majority of the floating plants, the Fairy Mosses are not very striking, but their green fern-like leaves turn red in the autumn, before dying out completely at the approach of winter. The next generation results from spores, which remain dormant until the spring. A larger species sometimes available is *A. filiculoides* which is a native of the South American Andes.

Eichhornia crassipes (**Floating Water Hyacinth**) The enlarged stems to the leaves of the Water Hyacinth contain cells filled with air, which give the plant its buoyancy. The trailing purplish roots are a favoured spawning site for goldfish, and pieces can subsequently be removed so the eggs can hatch safely. The attractive bluish flowers, with a distinct yellow spot on the uppermost petal, occur in groups at the top of a single spike, but are very short-lived.

Water Hyacinth will not survive the winter in the British climate, whereas in warmer parts of America, it can grow at such a rate that it becomes a serious pest, and its movement is banned in certain states for this reason. The plant is ideal for greenhouse ponds in temperate climates. Another form, *E. azurea*, with smaller bluer flowers, is also sometimes available. Its growth is generally less compact that *E. crassipes*.

Azolla filiculoides

Eichhornia crassipes

Hydrocharis morsusranae **(Frog-bit)** This plant has small, kidney-shaped, bright green leaves and white flowers. Frog-bit is easy to establish, just being allowed to float on the water's surface, but it will prove highly attractive to snails. Towards the end of the year, dormant buds fall off the plant, and sink to the bottom of the pond. They rise again during early summer, establishing the next generation to replace the previous plants which will have rotted away.

Lemna **(Duckweed)** There are various species of duckweed, the majority of which are not favoured by pond-keepers. The exception is the pale green Ivy-leaved form (*L. trisulca*). It only floats on the surface during the summer, providing shade and restricting algal growth in the pond itself for this period. Other species may become a major problem, especially in a large area of water, since duckweed can rapidly colonise most, if not all, of the pond's surface, outstripping the rate at which it can be eaten by the fish.

Lemna polyrhyza   *Stratiotes aloides*

Pistia stratiotes

Pistia stratiotes This is a plant which can only be grown in outdoor ponds in warmer climates. In shape and general appearance it resembles that of a garden lettuce.

Stratiotes aloides **(Water Soldier)** The Water Soldier rises to the water's surface just when it is about to flower. It has white blooms, set against spiky leaves in the form of a rosette, which resemble the upper part of a pineapple.

Trapa natans **(Water Chestnut)** There are in fact eight species in this genus, producing edible seed heads resembling chestnuts. They are annual plants. Since *Trapa* species are not very hardy, it may well be necessary to start them from seed each year under artificial conditions. It is important that the seed is not allowed to dry out completely, as this may destroy it. They should be planted in a shallow dish and covered in water.

Water Chestnuts have triangular leaves which are supported at the water's surface by air-filled stems. The white flowers are followed by the black seed heads about the size of a chestnut. In mild localities, they can establish themselves successfully.

Plants introduce colour and variety to a water garden.

Water-lilies

Water-lilies are the most decorative of the aquatic plants, and will flower over a relatively long period, depending on their environment. They are divided into two categories. The hardy water-lilies will do well under a wide range of growing conditions whereas the tropical species have to be kept in warmer surroundings. Lilies of this latter type can only be grown reliably in Britain and similar temperate countries if they are housed under glass.

There is a dazzling array of colour now available, as a whole range of vigorous hybrids have been established successfully. The following selection of hardy species given here is based on the depth of water which they require, and within each group, various colours are available.

Depth: 15-30 cm (6-12 ins)

The smallest lilies can be grown in shallow water, even sunken sinks, providing sufficient space is available at the surface, since they may spread over 40 cm (15 ins).

Nymphaea pygmaea alba   A variety with white flowers.

Nymphaea pygmaea hevola   Yellow flowers offset against mottled leaves.

Nymphaea pygmaea rubra   Slightly larger than the two previous lilies. The flowers are pinkish at first, turning darker as they mature. The leaves are green. Thought to have occurred as a natural hybrid.

Nymphaea odorata minor   A North American group of lilies, this form has white flowers with a noticeable scent, which reach a size of about 7.5 cm (3 ins). The leaves have a similar diameter, and are green on their upper surface and red below.

Depth: 30-45 cm (12-18 ins)

Nymphaea candida   A native plant in parts of north Europe, as well as Asia. It has white flowers with yellow centres, and grows well in tubs.

Nymphaea 'Aurora'   The flowers of this lily are yellowish at first, before turning orange and then dark red.

Water lilies come in many varieties and colours.

Nymphaea **'Paul Hariot'**   Another lily whose flowers change in colour as they mature, resembling 'Aurora' in this respect. It flowers freely, and produces relatively large blooms compared to foliage.

Nymphaea **'Ellisiana'**   Rich red flowers, with dark centres make this unusual lily a striking attraction to any pond.

Depth: 45-60 cm (18-24 ins)

Nymphaea laydekeri lilacea   The flowers are cup-shaped in appearance, changing gradually from a rosy lilac to carmine. This lily has dark green leaves.

Nymphaea laydekeri purpurata   The red flowers are relatively large compared to other *laydekeri* lilies, as are the leaves. It flowers readily throughout the summer.

Nymphaea laydekeri fulgens   One of the most striking lilies, it has deep red flowers produced in profusion, which may reach 10 cm (4 ins) in diameter. The leaves are green.

Nymphaea odorata sulphurea   This lily has yellow flowers, which are set relatively high from the water's surface, somewhat reminiscent of stars. The leaves have a mottled appearance with red spots on their lower face.

Nymphaea **'Albatross'**   Named after its white petals, which resemble birds about to fly. Albatross produces big flowers. Its leaves are purplish at first, turning green as they mature.

Depth: 60-90 cm (24-36 ins)

Nymphaea marliacea **'Albida'**   Another white variety, this is one of the easiest water-lilies to cultivate successfully. It grows freely as do other lilies of this species. The leaves are dark green, edged with brown. They show to best advantage in relatively large areas of water.

Nymphaea marliacea **'Chromatella'**   Like the previous variety, this is a robust, hardy lily which grows and flowers freely. Its blooms are pale yellow in colour, set against brown and green mottled leaves.

Nymphaea **'Conqueror'**   A red variety, which produces a profusion of blooms.

Many water lilies also have interestingly-coloured leaves.

Depth: Over 90 cm (36 ins)

Nymphaea **'Escarboule'**   Another French hybrid, some consider this the best of all the lilies, irrespective of their colour. It is undoubtedly the most perfect red variety, combining both size and shape with depth of coloration.

Nymphaea **'Sunrise'**   A genuine rich yellow lily, whose flowers may reach a diameter of 25 cm (10 ins). The petals are curved away from the water. Other varieties are sometimes sold under this name, but for Sunrise the leaves must be green on top and reddish-brown below. The stems are covered in characteristic hairs.

Nymphaea **'Gladstoniana'**   It is essential that this lily is only grown in deep water, otherwise its foliage may cover the striking white flowers, which can be 20 cm (8 ins) across.

Nymphaea tuberosa rosea   This is a fragrant, pink-flowered lily. It requires similar conditions to other members of the group.

A beautiful white water-lily about to open.

There are many other varieties of water-lily available, with the foregoing being just a selection of the most common, hardy types. Reference should be made to one of the more specialist books listed in the bibliography for further information on particular varieties. Most nurseries selling lilies will be able to advise on the requirements of their particular stocks.

Tropical water lilies

This group of lilies is available in a much wider range of colours, producing bigger and more fragrant blooms than their hardy counterparts. Some varieties flower at night whereas others close at dusk. It is occasionally possible to cultivate them successfully out of doors in mild parts of Britain, where the temperature will not fall below 18°C (65°F). Alternatively, they will have to be grown inside.

Certain members of the group have an interesting means of reproduction, whereby they develop complete miniature plants with tiny bulbs on their leaves. These can then be detached and rooted separately. Water-lilies of this type are decribed as viviparous, and are considered the hardiest members of the tropical group.

They include Isabella Pring, which will produce snow white flowers with yellow stamens in the centre. It has an attractive fragrance. One of the biggest, complete with sky blue blooms, is Margaret Rendig. A similar blue form is Mrs Martin E. Randig, the blooms of which will change in colour from mauve to purple as they mature. Its leaves are green, with brownish undersides. Royal Purple is much darker in colour, producing deep purple flowers.

Panama Pacific is another variety whose colour changes. Its rich red flowers turn more purplish with age. Peach Blow has pink petals, with a yellow base to its stamens. Pink Platter is similar in colour, although the flowers have long narrow petals, tapering to a relatively sharp point. Talisman has pale yellow blooms, with a pinkish tinge at first, but gradually their colour deepens, and the pink coloration extends over a wider area.

Night blooming tropicals

The flowers of these water-lilies open at dusk, and are generally closed by noon the next day. Their fragrance and colour are most conspicuous features. The type known as Mrs George C. Hitchcock produces some of the largest flowers, which can be 35 cm (14 ins) across and are deep pink in colour. H. C. Haarstick is a lily which has just slightly smaller red flowers, but is an equally strong grower, and will also flower consistently. Another red lily of this type is Red Flare, which also has distinctive mahogany red leaves. Two of the most popular white lilies are called Missouri and Sir Galahad. The former variety is of a more creamy shade, and generally blooms less profusely.

Planting the pond

Here are some guidelines when planning the numbers of plants required for a given area. A single marginal plant and lily should be allowed for each 1.8-2.3 square metres (20-25 square feet) of water surface. In the case of oxygenators, the number of plants required can be calculated on the basis of one for each .18 square metres (2 square feet), although for a pond with a total area exceeding 3.7 square metres (40 square feet), an allowance of one plant per .37 square metres (4 square feet) will suffice.

Plants for the pond can be purchased either from a local dealer or by mail from a specialist nursery. The latter may be necessary when seeking a particular variety of water-lily, for example. Under these circumstance, if a collection of plants is ordered, they will be packed separately and clearly labelled with growing instructions, so there will be no risk of muddling them. The planting season is relatively short, only extending from April to early September in Britain. Moving such plants outside this period, when they are dormant, will cause them to rot.

The plants themselves, with the exception of floating species which are just dropped onto the water's surface, should be set in containers. This will help to restrict the spread of more invasive plants, while enabling them to be moved easily. Special plastic planting baskets are available for this purpose. They are very durable, and although occasionally they may be split by the corm of a water-lily, they will otherwise last for years. The sides are perforated, ensuring that the plant roots can extract nutrients directly from the pond water. The size of the basket will be determined by the plants which are to be grown. Three sizes are normally available, the largest of which, measuring about 30 × 30 × 20 cm (12 × 12 × 8 ins) will accommodate a single lily or a dozen oxygenators. The medium size of basket will accommodate a maximum of two marginal plants or up to ten oxygenators. Only a *pygmaea* lily, a single marginal, or about half a dozen oxygenators should be planted in the smallest containers, which are about 20 × 20 × 10 cm (8 × 8 × 4 ins).

Before actually putting the plants in their baskets, they must be thoroughly cleaned by immersing them in a weak solution of potassium permanganate for three hours. Sufficient of the chemical just to turn the water pinkish will be required. Such treatment should overcome the risk of introducing either disease or unwanted parasites into the pond with the plants. After being removed from the potassium permanganate solution, they will need to be washed off thoroughly under a tap. Any dead or yellowing leaves should be removed at this stage.

The planting baskets must be lined with hessian sacking, and can then be filled with garden soil, up to a height of about 2.5 cm (1 inch) below the top of the container. While clay soil is preferable, manure or fertiliser should never be added to the planting medium, as they may prove detrimental to the fish. The plants can then be set in place, according to the instructions.

Oxygenators can simply be set in holes made with a pencil, and firmed into place. In the case of rooted plants, care should be taken to ensure that the roots are roughly spread out in the basket and not tightly bunched up in a clump.

With water-lilies, their roots can be trimmed back slightly if they are very long. The method of planting in this case depends on the variety concerned. The *odorata* group grow in the form of an elongated corm. These have to be buried about 2.5 cm (1 inch) below the surface of the soil with just the corm exposed. The *marliacea* lilies as well as tropical lilies are set vertically in the planting container, with the crown clearly visible above the soil. Although *laydekeri* resembles *marliacea* in appearance, it is set at more of an angle, closer to the horizontal.

Once the plants are in place, a thick layer of well-washed gravel should be placed on top of the earth, which will prevent the fish from digging in the soil, and possibly uprooting the plants. For persistent offenders, typically large koi, it may be necessary to use suitable stones to cover the surface of the earth.

The baskets should first be submerged in shallow water, so that air can be driven out and the soil saturated with water. A suitable basc will be necessary on which to stand the containers, so that the plants are not totally submerged from the outset. Limestone materials must not be used for this purpose, though, for reasons explained previously. The base will need to be adjustable, so as the plants grow they can be lowered until ultimately, in the case of lilies, their baskets will be at the base of the pond. Marginals remain confined to the marginal shelf, and are not positioned in the main body of water. Depth figures quoted always refer to the height of water directly above the plant, rather than including the depth of the container as well.

It is vital that the whole of the planting process is carried out with the minimum of delay. Plants out of water must be kept cool and preferably damp, being wrapped in sodden newspaper, for example. While floating plants require very little attention, it is not unusual for certain species, such as the Water Soldier, to sink when first put in the pond. They should soon rise again.

Plant pests

Various insects may attack plants growing within the confines of the pond. The Brown China Mark Moth (*Nymphula*) lays its eggs on the aquatic vegetation, and the resultant caterpillars will eat the leaves. It is not safe to use any sprays to control such pests, and apart from taking the caterpillars off individually and feeding them to the fish, the only alternative is to remove affected leaves.

The Water-Lily Beetle (*Galerucella grisescens*) is not encountered very often, and can be controlled by removing damaged leaves, with the larvae.

Water-Lily Aphids (*Rhopalosiphum*) may accumulate in large numbers on certain plants, and are hard to deter successfully, short of wiping them off the individual leaves.

Fish for ponds

Fish add movement and colour to what can otherwise be a fairly static scene, and various species are suitable for a pond. The choice will be influenced by the compatability and price of the fish, as well as the size of the pond. It is vital not to overstock the pond, and as a rough guide, the maximum should be 5 cm of fish per 30 square centimetres (2 ins of fish per square foot) of pond surface. It is the surface area, rather than the depth which is important for fish, since this is where oxygen enters the water.

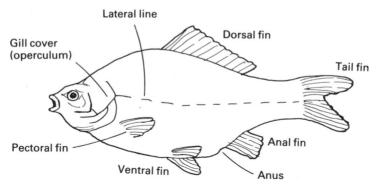

Topography of a fish

Bitterling (*Rhodeus amarus*)

The Bitterling makes an interesting addition to a pond. It occurs naturally in Central Europe and Russia, and grows to a maximum length of 6.5 cm (2½ ins). These fish are predominantly silver in colour, although during the breeding season, male fish take on a resplendent hue of violet, blue and red marking. Females develop an egg-laying tube called an ovipositor which itself can be 5 cm (2 ins) in length.

Bitterling

Swan Mussel

Breeding will only be successful if swan mussels are also present in the pond. The female Bitterling lays her eggs directly into the mussel, while her mate hovers close by to fertilise them. His milt is actually sucked into the mussel through its intake siphon. The young fish ultimately hatch inside the mussel, and escape from its relative safe confines through the siphon. The mussel in turn may use the fish as hosts for its parasitic offspring, known as *glochidia*. (The requirements of swan mussels are considered on page 86).

Carp (*Cyprinus* species)

The Common Carp will live well under pond conditions, but is not very colourful. These fish also grow to a large size, perhaps 60 cm (2 feet) in length, and can hybridise with goldfish. Two distinctive forms are recognised. The Leather Carp resembles the matt form of the goldfish, having a very dull appearance, whereas the Mirror Carp has one or two rows of greatly enlarged scales either side of its body, which are similar to a mirror.

The Crucian Carp (*C. carassius*) is a native of Asia, and is smaller, rarely attaining 37.5 cm (15 ins) in length. It appears greenish-brown when viewed from above, although its sides and underparts are paler in colour. Unlike the Common Carp, it does not have barbels around the mouth.

Certain forms of the carp, apart from the goldfish, have been bred for ornamental purposes in the East. The Golden Carp, or Hi-goi, is a colour variant of the Common Carp which first appeared in China and was then introduced to Japan. As its name suggests, it has a more yellowish appearance overall, but is similar in other respects. Although these fish can reach a size of 50 cm (20 ins), they do not often exceed 25 cm (10 ins) in most ponds. The growth of fish is influenced to a certain extent by the space available to them, with those kept in relatively small surroundings often remaining quite dwarfed. Golden Carp are not always easy to obtain compared to some pond fish, and may have to be acquired from more specialised dealers.

Koi are without doubt the most striking and spectacular of the larger ornamental carp, and have attracted much attention from western aquarists during recent years. These fish were first bred in Japan, derived from Common Carp being kept for food. In northern parts of that country the winters were too severe to farm carp successfully out of doors, and so their pools were enlarged to form part of the human dwelling where heat was available. Colour mutants of the fish emerged, and the carp farmers soon started selectively breeding and arranging shows for such carp.

Koi Carp

The red and white form, referred to as *Kohaku*, which is still the most popular variety in Japan today, was firmly established by 1870. Hybridisation with Leather and Mirror Carp sent in 1904 from Germany gave rise to the various scale types now in existence. Such fish are described as '*Doitsu*', which is the Japanese word for 'German'.

The emerging strains of ornamental carp were first named following an exhibition held in Tokyo, being referred to as *Nishikigoi*, meaning Brocaded or Colourful Carp. Breeders have since devoted years to produce particularly colour forms. It took Sawata Aoki a quarter of a century to breed the bright golden type known as *Ohgon*. Subsequently, an orange form, *Orenfii Ohgon* and yellow koi, described as *Yamabuki Ohgon*, after the flowers of a shrub, have also been established. The term 'koi' is corrupted from the Japanese word 'goi', which simply means carp. Some of the more common forms are listed below.

Name	Brief description
Shiro Muji	White
Aka Muji	Red
Shiro Bekko	White with black spots
Aka Bekko	Red with black spots
Tancho	White body with red head
Ki Utsuri	Black body with yellow markings
Kin Utsuri	Black body with golden markings
Hi Utsuri	Black body with red markings
Shiro Utsuri	Black body with white markings
Kin Ki Utsuri	Black and yellow, with some bright scales
Cha Goi	Brown
Ki Goi	Yellow
Taisho Sanke	White overlaid with black and red. Colours must not overlap
Kin Kaluto	Golden 'helmet' on head

Although very appealing, both on grounds of their colour and potential for taming, koi are demanding fish, and a pond will need to be designed with their requirements uppermost, rather than simply placing them in an established set-up. They are big, active fish, often growing to 60 cm (2 feet) or more in length, and need correspondingly large surroundings. A pond for them should be about 3 metres (10 feet) long, and at least 1.2 metres (4 feet) in depth to overwinter them successfully. In common with other carp, koi are bottom-feeders, and spend a lot of time stirring up detrius from the bottom of the pond. A filtration system is therefore essential, especially as their beauty cannot be appreciated when they are in murky water.

Koi grow quickly, and need a large amount of food to sustain their growth. They generally browse remorselessly on vegetation, and are not usually kept in planted pools as a result, although water-lilies may be sufficiently tough to deter their attention.

Such is the interest in koi that a specialist club, known as the British Koi Keepers' Society was formed during 1970, and now has a large membership, catering for all those interested in these magnificent carp whether just as pond fish or for exhibition purposes. Well-marked specimens can be extremely valuable. More details on koi can be obtained from some of the specialist books listed in the bibliography.

Goldfish (*Carassius auratus*)

The Goldfish, another member of the Cyprinidae, remains the most obvious choice for the outdoor pond, although not all varieties are sufficiently hardy to live outside throughout the year. These fish show to good advantage when viewed from above, whereas other fish have evolved dark backs as a means of protection from predators, and so are not as conspicuous.

The Common Goldfish is the original mutant, thought to have been first bred about AD 800 in China. These fish can in fact be quite variable in colour, ranging from a deep reddish-orange through yellow to silver. Immature goldfish are olive-black until they acquire their adult colouring. Any showing sporadic areas of black will lose this feature.

Common Goldfish are just one of the many varieties which are now established. The London Shubunkin resembles the Common Goldfish in shape, but differs in its scale structure. In the case of the metallic fish, iridocytes beneath the scales reflect light back, giving them their shiny appearance. Shubunkins in contrast have smaller number of these cells, and thus their appearance is altered. This scale type is referred to as 'nacreous' or sometimes by the older description of 'calico'. Such fish appear speckled, resembling mother-of-pearl, and no two individuals have identical markings. Their scaling can be a combination of red, orange, white, brown and even blue in some cases.

Shubunkins are divided into two categories. The London form is simply the nacreous counterpart of the Common Goldfish, whereas the Bristol Shubunkin has more elaborate fins, and a relatively streamlined body. Both these forms, as their names suggest, originated in Britain. The London Shubunkin can reach a size of 25 cm (10 ins) or so.

Comets were first bred during the 1880s in America, and are characterised by their elongated fins which taper to a point. The caudal, or tail, fin is prominently forked. These are active goldfish which do best under pond conditions and they are powerful swimmers. They are available in a similar range of colours to the Common Goldfish, with the red and white form, sometimes described as the 'Sarasso Comet', often most commonly available.

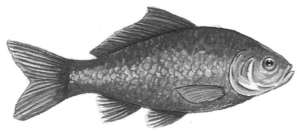

Goldfish

Shubunkin

Comet

While the foregoing varieties should all survive in a pond over the winter, there are others which can only be kept under such conditions for the warmer summer months, alongside their hardier counterparts. The Moor, which is jet black in colour will show up its colourful relatives well. The Fantail can be considered the most hardy of the various goldfish with elaborate fins. Like the Moor, it has a relatively corpulent body, less streamlined than those of the previous varieties. Fantails only grow to about 10 cm (4 ins) in size, and are named after their enlarged, paired tail fins. Forms of the Fantail and Moor which have very prominent eyes, described as 'telescope-eyed' are not recommended for a pond environment, while Goldfish with such elaborate finnage are liable to develop fin congestion when kept in cold water.

Gudgeon (*Gobio gobio*)

The Gudgeon is a relatively small member of the Carp family. It is greyish-brown in colour, with lighter sides transversed by bluish-black spots. The eyes are quite prominent, and there are two distinctive barbels extending downwards from its mouth. Gregarious by nature, the gudgeon will not harm other fish, although being omnivorous in its feeding habits, young fry may occasionally be taken. Their own eggs are laid in batches on the floor of the pond, and should hatch after about ten days. Gudgeon can be tamed quite easily, especially if fed in the same spot each day.

Minnow (*Phoxinus phoxinus*)

These are small fish, generally less than 15 cm (6 ins) in size, with a wide distribution throughout much of Britain and Ireland. Minnows occur in shoals, usually in rivers·and similar clear water locations, darting away readily at any hint of danger. They have green-brown backs, with silvery-greyish sides broken by darker barring. When in breeding condition, males can be recognised by their scarlet bellies, as is also the case with Sticklebacks. A good supply of live food will achieve this aim.

Minnow

Orfe (*Idus idus*)

The Orfe is a European fish which grows fast and requires a spacious environment. It can attain a size of 50 cm (20 ins) or more. The golden type is generally considered to be the most attractive form of this fish. It is a brilliant gold colour, becoming pinkish-silver on the underparts. The natural Silver Orfe is greyish-black when seen from above, paler on the sides and with a silvery tint to its belly. This is not, therefore, a particularly conspicuous fish, although Orfe are active by nature and frequently feed at the surface.

During the summer, Orfe will lurk in the upper reaches of the water, leaping up to catch midges and similar creatures which venture too close. Livefood is, in fact, an important item in their diet, although they are not fastidious feeders. They breed in a similar manner to goldfish, but produce larger eggs. The young fish attain their coloration relatively quickly, losing the dark markings on their heads as they mature. It is vital, however, not to overcrowd Orfe, since they are very susceptible to a shortage of oxygen in the water, and may well succumb in stormy weather for this reason. A pond fed by a waterfall, or with a fountain, will overcome the problem to some extent, as this will improve the circulation and oxygenation of water in the pond.

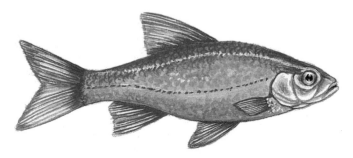

Golden Orfe

Roach (*Rutilus rutilus*)

The Roach occurs naturally in certain parts of Britain, as well as Ireland, where it is confined to the Blackwater River. These fish prefer quiet stretches of water, such as canals and ponds.

Roach are not especially colourful, although their fins are reddish. They are social fish by nature, congregating to spawn during early spring, with the pale green eggs being laid at the bottom of the pond. The fry then hatch in about ten days or so, and seek shelter amongst neighbouring vegetation in shallow water.

Roach are not particularly popular as pond fish, having acquired a reputation for being susceptible to fungal infections. The colour and greater hardiness of its relative the Rudd have penalised the Roach in this respect.

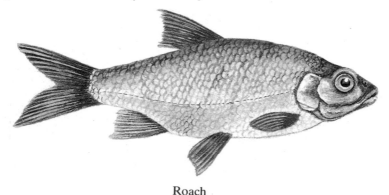

Roach

Rudd (*Scardinius erythropthalmus*)

The Rudd is found in similar habitats to the Roach. They are nimble swimmers, at home in slow, weedy water, often spending much of their time near the surface, and normally occurring in shoals. Two colour types are recognised. The golden form has a brownish back, with reddish-gold sides and bright red fins. Silver Rudd in contrast are less colourful, with silverish flanks. Rudd will often breed quite well in ponds.

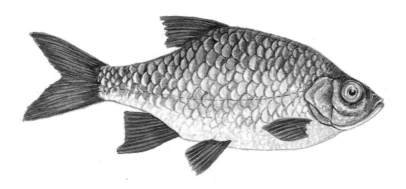

Rudd

Sticklebacks (*Gasterosteus* species)

Sticklebacks are only small fish, growing to a size of 5 cm (2 ins) or so, but they have an aggressive nature, which becomes especially evident during the breeding season. Each male constructs a nest, and then drives a number of females into it, where the eggs are fertilised. He then guards them until they hatch, driving off potential rivals or other fish which approach too closely. Found throughout much of Britain as well as America, Sticklebacks have highly predatory natures, feeding almost exclusively on livefoods, including fish spawn and fry. In view of these characteristics, it is advisable not to include them in a pond with other fish.

Stone Loach (*Cobitis barbatula*)

The loaches are a group of fish closely related to the Carps. The Stone Loach is quite a common species in waters throughout Britain, being brownish-green in colour with white underparts. It has six barbels attaching on or close to the mouth, and spends much of its time hiding under rocks or similar sites. Stone Loaches are therefore not very conspicuous pond occupants, but.will prove useful scavengers.

Stone Loach

Tench (*Tinca tinca*)

The Tench is another useful fish to have in a pond because of its scavenging habits. The golden form is once again most conspicuous, although tench generally spend more time in deeper water than other fish. During the day, they often lurk near the bottom of the pond, and feed especially at night.

Tench are characterised by their minute scales, and have barbels, acting as sensory devices, at the corner of each side of the mouth to assist them in locating food under murky conditions. This fish has a roundish appearance overall, both

61

with regard to its body shape and fins. Tench feel slimy to the touch because of a thick protective mucus layer over the surface of their bodies. The wild form of the Tench is known as the green, apart from the more attractive golden variety.

These fish will breed quite well in a relatively large pond, although they spawn later in the year than most other species. Their eggs fix to plants, and hatch in about a week. The young fish are green with a golden hue, and have blue markings on the throat. They in turn can breed during their second year, and may grow to more than 50 cm (20 ins). In the average pond, however, tench rarely grow much bigger than 15 cm (6 ins), and can be kept safely alonside other fish.

Tench

Fish to avoid

While the foregoing gives an indication of the most popular species for the pond, there are certain fish which should be avoided. Catfish fall in this category. The European species, *Silurus glanis*, is frequently available, and often in view of its small size, may seem innocuous. These fish will soon grow, however, at the expense of other pond occupants since they are highly predatory. The American Catfish (*Ameiurus nebulosus*) has similar habits, and additionally can cause a nasty injury with its sharp spines if handled carelessly.

Obtaining fish

The source of supply will be dependent largely upon the species concerned. Goldfish are freely available from many pet stores, aquarist dealers and garden centres during the spring and early summer. A significant proportion of these fish will have been imported, often from countries in the Far East where they are bred commercially. Home-bred stock is preferable, however, even if slightly more expensive, since it will not have undergone such drastic changes in environment.

It may be possible to catch fish for the pond from the wild, depending on the area concerned. Pigmy Sunfish (*Elassama evergladei*), which do well under American conditions, inhabit areas of water from North Carolina to the everglades of Florida. Two related species (*E. zonatum* and *E. akefenakee*) have a similar distribution. As its name suggests, the Pigmy Sunfish only reaches a size of about 38 mm (1½ ins). There is always a risk of introducing disease from such wild-caught fish, and indeed all fish should be quarantined for at least two weeks before they are introduced to the pond. This also applies to new fish which are to be added to an existing pond.

In separate quarters, any disease can be dealt with quite effectively; treatment and control is likely to be much more costly and difficult in the pond itself. Fish, as with all creatures, are especially likely to succumb to illness when stressed. Moving them from a fish farm, and then distributing them, possibly not even direct to the retail dealer, is likely to mean that they may be undernourished as a result.

Healthy fish have active, alert natures and swim with their fins held erect, and any which appear off-colour are best avoided. Fish with ragged or drooping fins are liable to be a source of problems, as are individuals with a whitish film over their eyes. Those showing signs of damage to their bodies, in the form of lost scales, ulcers or white spots should not be purchased, and others in their company need to be viewed with suspicion if the complaint is contagious. Fungal infections often develop following only superficial damage to the body.

Quarantine

Having established the pond, it is vital to take every possible precaution to eliminate the risk of disease. Simple, cheap quarantine quarters for fish can be set up using a children's inflatable paddling pool, which will have no sharp edges where they could damage themselves if frightened. When not in use, it can be deflated, dried and stored in a small area. As an alternative, a pond liner can be fixed over a wooden or wire frame, taking care to ensure that no nails or ends of wire penetrate the liner. An aquarium of suitable size offers another possibility for quarantine quarters.

The top of the chosen container must be covered to prevent the fish jumping out. Koi are particularly agile in this respect, and may leap out with little difficulty. Soft fruit netting can be used for the purpose, if weighted down around the sides of the temporary pool with blocks. This will also serve to protect the fish from possible predators, such as cats or even herons. It is important to use a soft netting, since the fish may still injure themselves just by coming into contact with it. For this reason, some people prefer to construct a high fencing surround, rather than actually netting over the water surface. The problem is unlikely to arise when the fish are in the pond itself, since there will be hiding places and a greater depth of water, enabling them to retreat if they feel threatened.

The quarantine pool should be filled several days before the fish are acquired. This time gap will allow the chlorine in the water to be dissipated. Even minute quantities of this chemical in the water will be toxic to the fish. On arrival home, they should be tipped very gently out of the bag or bucket used to transport them into the water of their temporary accommodation. It is not strictly necessary with cold-water fish to float the bag on the water surface for 20 minutes or so to allow the water temperature to equilibrate unless there is likely to be a marked difference in this respect.

Feeding fish

Fish nutrition has advanced greatly during recent years, away from diets based almost exclusively on dried ants' eggs, which are of little value. The ingredients which fish require in their food are basically the same as those necessary to ensure a balanced diet for humans. Proteins are important for growth, carbohydrate for energy, and fat stores are important for successful overwintering, when the fishes' appetites are depressed. Vitamins and minerals must also be present in the diet, fulfilling a number of diverse roles, ranging from ensuring a healthy skeletal system to being actively involved in the digestive process.

Complete diets for fish are divided into flaked and pelleted rations. The latter is preferable, since pellets will float for quite a long period, and attract the fish to the surface. Flaked foods sink relatively quickly, but are just as palatable. Feeding time affords an opportunity to study the fish, and note any which appear to be ailing. It is important not to overfeed them, since excess pellets will pollute the water. Certain fish, such as koi, can become very tame, and will learn to feed almost directly from the hand, if food is offered at the same place and time each day.

The appetite of the fish will vary depending on the time of year. During the warmer months, they will need feeding perhaps three times a day, whereas when the water temperature declines, so will their appetite. There is normally a brief increase in food consumption during the autumn, however, enabling the fish to increase body fat stores which will sustain them over the winter period. They stop feeding completely once the water temperature goes down to about 5°C (40°F), and their digestive processes cease to function as well. It is therefore often considered dangerous to offer food over the winter period, even if the weather turns warm, stirring the fish out of their torpid state, since it will probably remain undigested in the gut.

At the approach of spring, the fish will gradually start to eat again and it is usual to provide livefood at this stage, which will help to bring them into breeding condition. There are various types of livefood which can be fed to fish, and some of these can be cultivated artificially. Those of aquatic origin are viewed with suspicion by some fish-keepers since it is possible to introduce disease and unwanted parasites into the pond through such items.

Nevertheless, the two most readily-obtainable livefoods are tubifex and daphnia, both of which can be purchased from most aquarist stores. Tubifex are small worms occurring in silt where there are high levels of organic matter present in the immediate surroundings. Sewerage outfalls are common sites for such worms, and they can be collected when the water-level is low. Before being sold, they are washed very thoroughly and may be kept in a shallow tray or bowl of water in a cool spot for a day or so before feeding, so they can void their gut contents. Providing the water is changed on a daily basis, they will live under such conditions for over a week. Any which are uneaten in the pond may establish themselves in the silt at its base, forming a colony which will be attacked especially by bottom-feeding fish.

Daphnia, also known as Water Fleas, although they are minute crustaceans not related to fleas, occur naturally in many stagnant areas of water during the warmer months of the year. Here they can be caught using very fine nets, or alternatively, may be purchased in bags. Only bags containing a high proportion of live daphnia should be obtained, and although relatively expensive, they are of particular benefit to fish in the spring.

The major danger of feeding daphnia is that other, harmful creatures will be introduced with them into the pond. For this reason, a set of special fine sieves should be acquired, so that the water can be run off separately while the daphnia are retained in the sieve. It is then possible to examine them closely, in case leeches and other pests are also present. These can then be removed with tweezers before the daphnia are released into the pond.

During the summer, a variety of winged insects will be attracted to the water, laying their eggs in the pond. The larvae of midges, known as bloodworms because of their red coloration, are a popular fish food. Glassworms, also the larval stage of a midge and not a worm at all, are most active at night, and can be collected from many pools in the late evening.

Mosquito larvae are one of the easiest livefoods of this type to gather since they remain near the water's surface for much of the time, although they are very sensitive to any movement in their vicinity. As with similar livefoods they can be caught in a fine-meshed net, with the catch being inspected before it is tipped into the pond for the fish. Adult female mosquitos can be attracted to lay their eggs by leaving shallow trays of water out in the open in fairly shady surroundings. The larvae are easily caught by pouring off the water through an appropriately fine net, and there should be no risk of introducing other creatures by this means.

Certain livefoods are only suitable for relatively large fish. The Freshwater Shrimp (*Gammarus*) can be caught in areas of flowing water where there is also plenty of vegetation. They are often found joined together in pairs or with young attached. Their tough, protective exoskeleton means that they are only suitable for big fish. The Water Woodlouse (*Asellus*) has a similarly hard outer covering to its body. In a pond alongside amphibians, fish may also feed on frog tadpoles, although those of newts and toads are usually ignored.

Incorporating a bridge into the garden allows good access for watching fish.

Terrestrial livefoods

In order to overcome the potential problems associated with the use of aquatic livefoods, there are several ideal substitutes, some of which can be cultured with the minimum of difficulty to ensure a constant supply is available. Earthworms have long been regarded as perhaps the best conditioning food for fish, although they have to be cut up prior to feeding, which is an unpleasant task. Those gathered in the garden should be left in damp grass for a day or so, so they can empty their gut contents. Smaller worms are generally preferable, and they can be purchased from bait dealers if required.

It should not be necessary to dig the garden continually in search of worms, as they can be encouraged to congregate in a particular area. Worms will be drawn to the surface by placing a layer of black polythene or hessian on well-watered soil, covering vegetable matter or even tea leaves. After a day or so, particularly during a period of dry weather, the worms can be removed when the sacking is lifted back. Worms around manure heaps are best avoided as a source of fish food.

Whiteworms (*Enchytraeus*) are relatively small, attaining a maximum size of about 1.9 cm (¾ inch). Starter cultures can be purchased from a local aquarist store, or by mail order if necessary. These worms should be housed in a suitable container, such as a disused margarine tub with hole punched in the lid. They need damp surroundings, and so the base should be lined with a mixture of damp peat and soil. The starter culture must be split into several groups, each of which are buried in the peat mixture. Bread soaked in milk, or cooked oatmeal, will suffice for feeding purposes, with the culture being placed in a temperature of 15°-20°C (58°-68°F). The worms develop in clumps, and after about a month can be harvested from the culture with forceps. Any uneaten food must be replaced every couple of days, and other cultures can be set up as needed.

There are other, even smaller worms which are very similar to whiteworms in their requirements, and thus ideal for young fish. Grindal worms for example will do well in shallower surroundings, but require a high temperature, about 21°C (70°F), and multiply rapidly. Microworms are even smaller, about 3 mm (⅛ inch) in size. Cultures of these worms tend to sour quite quickly and therefore have to be restarted each week. A cereal food, mixed to the consistency of a paste and smeared over the bottom of their container will provide nutriment for the worms, which are simply placed on top. The culture should then be covered with glass and left at room temperature. The worms can be collected within a couple of days, and washed off before being fed to the fish. Microworms are of particular value for smaller, growing fish.

Maggots are another livefood which can be cultured, but it is better to acquire them from a bait shop. The smaller brand, which have not been artificially dyed, make the best fish food. Their hard outer casing will be discarded. Prior to feeding, the maggots must be kept in a cool place, otherwise they will rapidly pupate and emerge as adult flies.

Freeze-dried foods

Such items offer a useful alternative when no livefoods are available. The processing ensures that they retain both their palatability and nutritional value, and can be stored without refrigeration for an indefinite period. As with other prepared foods such as pellets, they must be kept dry, in an air-tight container. Amongst the livefoods available in this form are tubifex, bloodworms and daphnia.

Another development in fish feeding has been the introduction of irradiated foodstuffs, free from disease yet with vitamins added. A wide range of foods are now processed by this means, ranging from lobster to bloodworms. These must be kept frozen, then allowed to thaw out completely before being offered to the fish.

Summary

A wide range of possible options are now available when feeding fish, and variety in their diet is recommended. Complete fish foods in the form of pellets should be supplemented whenever possible by livefood in one form or another. Fish such as koi which will browse readily on growing vegetation in the pond, can be distracted by the provision of boiled spinach or lettuce leaves as palatable alternatives. Various other items, ranging from scrambled egg to oatmeal and even cooked heart, chopped into small pieces with all fat removed, are usually acceptable to fish. Indeed, some fish-keepers still mix up their own particular diets with such ingredients, but since there is an adequate choice of prepared foods now available, containing all the essential ingredients in adequate proportions, this is no longer necessary.

Breeding fish in ponds

In the surroundings of a pond, it is obviously not possible to keep such a close watch on the fish, and generally breeding under these conditions leads to less fry being reared than would be expected in an aquarium. Yet, with a well-planted pond, breeding is quite likely to take place successfully, if the fish themselves are in good condition. Feeding plays an important part in this process, and as soon as the fish regain their appetites and become more active in the late spring, livefood should be offered regularly. Among the characteristic signs of breeding are changes in the appearance of the fish themselves. Females swell with roe, while males often undergo colour changes, becoming brighter. Sticklebacks develop their red bellies, while goldfish show tiny white pimples on the gill plates, extending up to the pectoral fins in some cases. These swellings should not be mistaken for the parasitic disease called white spot, which generally develops all over the body, rather than being confined to a particular area (see page 76).

The best time to watch for signs of spawning activity is during the early morning, especially when sunlight is falling on the water. This appears to act as a stimulant. The male will pursue the chosen female relentlessly, driving her into vegetation where the eggs will be laid and fertilised immediately.

Unfortunately, the eggs are then likely to be eaten by the fish themselves unless they are adequately hidden, or else removed. Goldfish, for example, may produce 500 or so eggs during a single spawning, yet such is the wastage of both eggs and the resulting fry than only a handful of young fish will ultimately survive.

In order to maximise on the number of fish reared, the eggs must therefore be transferred to a pool or aquarium on their own. The length of time taken to hatch is dependent on temperature, and it is common practice to use an aquarium heater to raise the water temperature up to a maximum of 24°C

(75°F). This will ensure that the eggs should hatch in three or four days, compared to a period of perhaps a fortnight or so in a pond. It is easiest to use a combined heater-thermostat unit for this purpose, in conjunction with a suitable thermometer. If the temperature rises above 24°C (75°F) the eggs may not hatch.

The tiny fry are not free-swimming when they emerge from their eggs, and remain inert for the first couple of days. During this period, they are sustained by the remains of their yolk sacs, while their air-bladders, which subsequently give them buoyancy, are developing. It is important that the fry are left undisturbed during this period, as without adequate buoyancy, they can drown.

Once their yolk sacs are exhausted, the fry will start to feed on microscopic protozoa called infusoria. A culture of these minute creatures can be simply set up using water from the pond, and adding crushed lettuce leaves or similar vegetable matter. The jar should be placed in a warm place, which will encourage the protozoa to multiply rapidly. A succession of cultures will ensure that there is no shortage of this vital rearing food, although if necessary, commercial substitutes are now available.

Infusoria are fed to the fry by means of a connecting piece of tubing, leading from the jar to the aquarium, with a clamp being used to regulate the flow rate. The jar itself must be positioned above the aquarium, and the flow can be started by sucking the water along the tubing, setting up a siphon drip-feed. In an established pond, infusoria will be present in the water, but there will probably be insufficient to support the large numbers of fry which can be expected if they hatch in an environment free from predators.

As the young fish grow, they can be offered brine shrimp larvae from about the age of a fortnight onwards. The larvae are hatched from eggs, only a relatively small quantity of which should be purchased at any time. They rapidly deteriorate when exposed to air, and hatchability will be seriously affected as a result. Detailed instructions for hatching the eggs are included with each pack, but heated, well-aerated salt water is an essential requirement. The larvae, which hatch from the eggs in about a day, are referred to as *nauplii*, and having been sieved out of their container, can be fed to the young fish.

Fry have very large appetites, and must have food constantly available. As they get older, other items can be introduced to their diet, such as small daphnia and hard-boiled egg, forced through muslin to ensure only fine particles are offered. This latter item must only be given in small amounts as any excess will rapidly pollute the water. Microworms and finely chopped whiteworm can also be fed to older fry.

As the fish grow, it is likely that some malformed individuals will become evident, and these should be removed and destroyed, preferably be being placed in a plastic bag, which is then sealed and firmly trodden on. This ensures a quick end for any fish which have to be destroyed, and is much more humane than flushing them away down a toilet since death under these circumstances is likely to be far from instantaneous, taking place at some point in the sewerage system.

Artificially induced spawning

Apart from letting the fish spawn naturally, it is possible to induce them to do so artificially. This will yield a large number of eggs, which can then be hatched under controlled conditions. The technique used is known as hand spawning and must only be carried out in fish which are actually ready to breed. Once they are seen chasing, the chosen pair can then be caught up carefully and removed from the pool. Two containers will be necessary, both of which must be filled beforehand with water from the pond. Suitable oxygenator plants must also be included in the spawning bowl itself.

When catching fish, rectangular nets are often easier to use in a pond than circular ones. Fish must always be handled extremely gently, and only with wet hands, to prevent damage to their scales, which otherwise is likely to precipitate a fungal infection or deep bruising of body tissue itself.

The male of the pair should be restrained in the left hand, directly over the water of the bowl containing the plants, while the female is left swimming in the other container. Using the right hand, gentle pressure will need to be exerted at a spot immediately in front of the anal opening of the male. This should stimulate the release of the milt which will fertilise the female's eggs.

The process is repeated with the female, who will be induced to spawn in a similar manner. Alternatively, she can be carefully restrained against the side of the bowl containing the milt, which should have the same effect. The adult fish can then be returned to the pond, while the water in the bowl should be gently swirled around to bring the milt into contact with the eggs. It is not vital to obtain the milt first, and some breeders prefer to add this second, as happens naturally, once the female has spawned. The plants, to which the eggs will have adhered, are then removed from the bowl, and transferred to the aquarium where they will hatch.

The technique, sometimes referred to as 'hand stripping' is very effective, ensuring that a very high proportion of the eggs are fertilised, and leads to much larger numbers of fry than could be expected if the fish are just left in the pond. In addition, a particular pair of fish can be bred together by this means, ensuring that the parentage of the offspring will be known.

Spawning precautions

When spawning, fish unfortunately tend to lose their natural fear, and are therefore easy prey for cats and herons. As a precaution, the pond can be netted over, using a light mesh, although this is likely to be rather unsightly at a time when the pond is coming to life again.

Herons in particular have become a major problem at some commercial fish farms, and so means of deterring them harmlessly have received considerable study. Lights are relatively ineffective, only keeping the birds away for a matter of days. Some fish enthusiasts have dummy herons around their ponds, but this can have the reverse effect of attracting an unpaired bird. The most useful means of avoiding fish losses to herons is to erect a basic string fence, set at a height of about 30 cm (1 foot) above the ground, around the pond's perimeter. Herons do not in fact settle directly in water, but on land close by. Touching the string will scare them off, especially if two such fences are put up in parallel, sited 30 cm (1 foot) apart. Wire should not be used for this purpose, since it could injure the bird.

Fish lay their eggs among the vegetation in the pond.

Fish diseases and treatments

Good husbandry of the fish plays a major part in preventing disease, as with all livestock. A well-designed pond, which is not overstocked is unlikely to be a source of problems. If the pond is too shallow or overcrowded though, the fish will be seen gasping at the water's surface, during hot weather in particular, and losses can be anticipated unless their environment is improved. Care must be taken to keep weedkillers, insecticides and similar chemicals well away from the pond, as most preparations of this type are poisonous to fish. Sprays can also be blown on to the water's surface, with fatal consequences.

If a fish appears off-colour, it should be removed immediately and placed in a treatment tank or pond. The chances of a successful recovery here will be much greater, and this will help to prevent the spread of disease to other pond occupants. Such accommodation also affords greater opportunity to observe the fish, and hopefully decide on the cause of the condition.

A variety of proprietary remedies for many fish ailments are now available from aquarist stores. These must be added to the water at the correct dilution. Overdosing will not speed the cure but increase the risk of adverse side-effects. Many of these remedies are refinements based on dyes such as methylene blue and malachite green, which were formerly widely used by fish-keepers. Cooking salt can also be useful for the treatment of certain diseases, notably fungus. Antibiotics, which are only available through a veterinarian in Britain, are being used increasingly to counter bacterial disease in fish.

Fish ailments

Body rot

Any ulceration of the body is especially severe in fish since they will suffer from rapid fluid loss leading to circulatory failure. A serious form of this disease, known as 'Hole in the Body' is both contagious and usually fatal. It was probably introduced with imported fish, and has killed many goldfish and koi. Antibiotic treatment will give the best hope of a cure.

Eye disorders

Cataracts are not uncommon, causing a whitish glaze which usually affects one eye only. It may result from a parasitic infection when the immature worms migrate to the eye. The life cycle of the parasite concerned involves snails, and for this reason some pond-keepers will not have molluscs in their ponds. Using one part of phenoxethol in nine parts of water may prove effective in destroying these parasites, with the fish being left in the solution until it appears to have recovered. To prevent further outbreaks, snails must be removed from the pond, although the adult worm itself lives in waterfowl.

Fish may occasionally be noted with a swollen eye, this complaint is referred to as exophthalmia or 'pop-eye' and is a relatively common disorder of carp, forming part of the so-called carp-dropsy syndrome. In these cases, the fish also has a swollen bloated appearance because of the dropsy.

Fin rot and the effects of cold

The signs of this disease are ragged, frayed edges to the fins while the fish itself appear dull. Various bacteria of the Gram negative group are the cause of such infections and long-finned varieties of goldfish will often develop this disease when left outside during cold weather. Antibiotics or phenoxethol should be used for treatment, while the conditions for the fish must also be improved.

Fin congestion may also become evident when the fish are in cold surroundings. Red streaking, especially of the caudal fin, will be noticeable. Another condition known as 'shimmies' is also indicative of low body temperature, or hypothermia. Affected fish remain stationary yet move their bodies from side to side. A gradual increase in the temperature of their water should revive them.

Fungus

Fish are very prone to fungal infections, which show up as areas on the body with a cotton-wool-like appearance. Infections of this type usually result after an injury, or as a result of careless handling. Newly acquired fish, and those which may have been injured during spawning, should be watched closely for signs of fungus. Fungal spores can be found in almost all supplies of pond water, but are unable to attack healthy fish.

Treatment of fungal infections can be effective, providing it is begun early. A salt solution, made up using 6 grams of salt per litre of water (1 oz per 1 gallon) should lead to a recovery if the fish are immersed for 30 minutes or so each day. As with all remedies, though, should the fish appear distressed during treatment, they must be removed at once. It is vital to ensure that the water temperature of the treatment bath is the same as that to which the fish were previously exposed. This can be simply checked using a suitable thermometer.

A disease which sometimes affects pond fish is erroneously

Well cared for fish make striking pond inhabitants.

referred to as 'mouth fungus' although the causal organism is a bacterium *Chondrococcus columnaris*. Fish with this complaint become dull and refuse to eat, as the bacteria actually erode the tissue around the mouth. Antibiotic treatment or phenoxethol can overcome the infection, if it is recognised at an early stage.

Parasites

A wide range of parasites may affect fish, ranging from minute protozoa to creatures such as *Argulus*, which will be visible attached to the side of the fish. It is vital to try and keep such pests out of the pond by quarantining new fish, and washing plants off thoroughly as recommended previously. Once parasites gain access to a pond, they can be extremely difficult to eradicate without actually draining the whole pond and removing all fish.

White spot or 'Ick', caused by the protozoan *Ichthyopthirius* is one of the most prevalent parasitic diseases, and although more common in tropical fish, it can be equally fatal to cold-water species. The parasite actually burrows into the skin, giving rise to the characteristic white spots all over the fish's body. Death results from the damage caused by these injuries, or a subsequent fungal infection. Once mature, the parasite leaves the fish, and gives rise to the next generation on the floor of the pond. Over a thousand immature tomites may result from each of the cysts, although these will die unless they make contact with another fish in a couple of days.

Treatment with a proprietary remedy usually has to be repeated at an interval of three or four days to destroy these parasites completely. Infected fish should be removed to a tank of dechlorinated fresh water, where there will be less risk of a fungal infection subsequently developing. Faced with an epidemic of white spot, all fish will have to be caught up and transferred elsewhere. In their absence, the tomites will be unable to find any hosts, and so the infection will die out naturally, and the fish, once recovered, can be returned after a minimum of ten days.

The Anchor Worm (*Lernia*) also attacks the side of the fish, resembling a piece of thread when *in situ*. Only the female is parasitic, and attaches by means of her so-called anchors. Anchor Worms can be destroyed by a concentrated potassium permanganate solution applied using a small paint brush. The resulting wound should be dabbed with iodine solution. It takes about two months for all stages of this parasite to die out if all the fish are removed from the pond.

Flukes can affect the skin or gills of fish, and are difficult to spot, since they are relatively small. Skin flukes will cause the fish to rub itself on rockwork in particular, as it tries to ease the irritation. Inflamed areas will become apparent on the body, and are likely to be colonised by fungi. When flukes affect the gills, the fish has difficulty in breathing, and is seen gasping, with the operculum stretched wide open.

Sensible precautions should keep flukes out of the pond, but if they do gain access, commercial remedies can be used to eradicate them. There are various other parasites such as leeches which may also be introduced to the pond, and these creatures are considered in more detail in the next chapter.

Red pest

This disease is prevalent where fish are being kept in overcrowded conditions, taking its name from the characteristic reddish appearance of the fish's belly. The blood vessels in this region become engorged, and there may be accompanying haemorrhage. The gills can also be affected in some cases. Treatment consists of improving the fishes' environment and ensuring adequate circulation of water.

Swim-bladder disorders

If the fish appears to be having difficulty in swimming to the surface, it is likely that its air-bladder is not functioning correctly. Once again, this can occur directly as a result of low temperature, while undigested food may be pressing on the organ, decreasing its size. Affected fish should be transferred to water of just sufficient depth to cover them adequately, and allowed to fast for a week. A specific condition, known as carp swim-bladder disease, is seen in young fish, whose air bladders fill with debris, leading to contraction in their functional capacities. The cause of this complaint is unclear at present, and there is no really effective treatment.

Tuberculosis

Piscine tuberculosis does not present a threat to human health, although it is a similar chronic disease. Fish lose weight over a period of time, becoming dull and anorexic, although there are other possible causes of such symptoms. Tuberculosis is, however, a contagious complaint, and affected individuals must be isolated at once.

When faced with an outbreak of disease where the losses are high, it is worthwhile to have a post mortem carried out to establish the cause of death. Specialist laboratories which undertake such investigations can be contacted through a veterinarian. Particular attention should be paid to packing instructions if dead fish are being despatched by post, although whenever possible they should be taken direct to the laboratory along with written notes about their history and environment.

Other pond life

Once the pond is set up, a variety of other creatures are likely to be attracted to it. Some of these must be discouraged, while the pond-keeper may actively choose to include others. In the case of amphibians (and also reptiles in the US) it should be noted, however, that legislation may prevent the collection of some or all species, depending on the area concerned. In addition, under the *Wildlife and Countryside Act 1981*, the deliberate release of non-native species in Great Britain is outlawed. Certain species of amphibian have been introduced in the past, and are now established in the country.

The common frog is attracted to ponds, especially for spawning.

Amphibians

Two orders of amphibians are represented in Britain. The newts comprise the Order Caudata, which are the tailed amphibians, whereas frogs and toads are classified together in the Order Salienta. Amphibians possess lungs, and may live on land for much of their time, although they always return to the water for breeding, which normally takes place in spring and early summer. Since the majority require a damp environment, however, they may not stray far from the pond. They are cold-blooded, like fish, and thus dependent on the environmental temperature to regulate that of their bodies. During the winter months therefore, they become torpid, and hibernate until the approach of spring.

Newts

Three species occur in Britain, and out of these, the Common Newt (*Triturus vulgaris*) has the most widespread distribution,

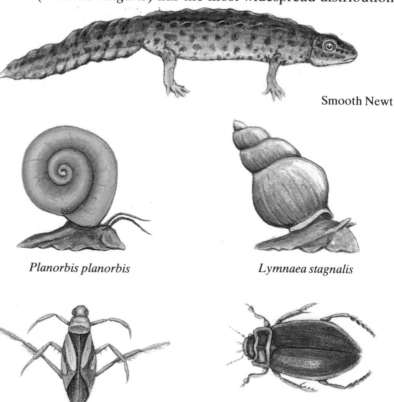

Smooth Newt

Planorbis planorbis

Lymnaea stagnalis

Water Boatman

Male *Dytiscus marginalis*

being found throughout much of the country. It grows to a size of about 10 cm (4 ins), and is fairly terrestrial in its habits. The sexes are discernible, since the male has an orangish-red belly, with black blotches over its body. Females in contrast are brownish in colour. In the spring, males develop a noticeable smooth ridge down their backs, while their body colour becomes more pronounced.

There is virtually no direct contact between pairs when they are mating. Male newts liberate a cone-shaped clear capsule of sperm into the water, close to their mates. The female is responsible for catching the capsule and holding it against her vent, thus enabling the sperm to escape. The eggs are therefore fertilised before they are laid. She deposits them singly on the undersurfaces of leaves, which may be bent over, helping to disguise the eggs during the crucial period when the tadpole is developing.

The young newts should emerge after about two weeks. They possess three distinct sets of feathery gills, which gradually reduce in size as the larvae begin to breathe air. As they grow, the forelegs start to develop first, followed by the hind limbs. During the late summer, some of these tadpoles will have changed into miniature newts, whereas others will not complete their metamorphosis until the following spring.

Palmate Newts (*T. helveticus*) resemble the Common Newt in appearance, although they are slightly smaller, only growing to about 7.5 cm (3 ins) in length. In areas where they overlap however, the Palmate Newt can generally be separated since it has less heavily spotted underparts, with no markings on the throat, which is pinkish in colour. When in breeding condition, male Palmates develop prominent webbing between the toes of their hind feet. A narrow filament also extends from the tip of the tail.

The Crested Newt (*T. cristatus*) is potentially the largest British species, and may range up to 17.5 cm (7 ins) in size. It has a predominantly black body, especially when living out of water. The colour of its belly ranges from yellowish to a deep red-orange shade. Males of this species have a very pronounced crest with a jagged edge during the breeding season. Their tails often develop whitish lines along the sides, while the skin itself has glands which produce an unpleasant substance which serves to deter potential predators. Crested Newts are often more aquatic than the previous species, being found in water for much of the year.

Alpine Newts (*T. alpestris*) are confined to the mainland of Europe, and are highly aquatic by nature. Indeed, in some areas, notably Yugoslavia, these newts may be encountered still possessing larval gills, even when they are mature. This species has a fairly distinctive appearance, with a dark central region running along the back. The sides of the body are spotted, while the underparts are reddish-orange. Alpine Newts are occasionally offered for sale in Britain.

One of the most common American species is the so-called Eastern Newt (*Notophthalmus iridescens*), which can be found on the eastern side of the country. Two larger species from the west coast are the Rough-skinned (*Taricha granulosa*) and Californian Newts (*T. torosa*). They are relatively similar in appearance, with the belly ranging from orange to red in colour, while the upperparts vary from brownish-red to black. Although largely terrestrial under normal circumstances, they can live quite successfully in water for much of the year.

Care of newts

Newts do not require any special care in a pond. They will feed on a variety of small livefoods, which can include their own offspring and other tadpoles as well as small fry. Chopped earthworm and whiteworm are popular foods, and if fed daily in the same place, newts can become relatively tame, awaiting their ration. The tadpoles are not difficult to rear when provided with suitable livefoods such as tubifex.

Frogs

Frogs and toads are known collectively as anurans. Only one species of frog is native to Britain, although two others have been introduced successfully in the past. The Common Frog (*Rana temporaria*) is in fact a highly terrestrial species of very variable coloration. It grows up to about 10 cm (4 ins), with older specimens having a relatively rounded snout. The webbing on the feet does not extend to the very tips of the toes, and the frog swims by means of its hind legs only. Common Frogs can range from pinkish-yellow to olive-brown in colour, with darker blotches and often black spots on the back. This species is usually only found in the pond during the breeding season, when males leap on and clasp the mates beneath them, gripping behind their front legs. The calls are especially noticeable at this time of year.

The so-called Edible Frog (*R. esculenta*) has been introduced to several localities in south-east England, but has not expanded its range significantly. It can attain a size of approximately 12.5 cm (5 ins), and is pale green in colour with black spots on its back which merge to form more distinct blotches on the thighs. The hind region of this part of the legs is usually orangish-yellow, while the males' vocal sacs are whitish. Edible Frogs are highly aquatic by nature, spending much of their time in water. It is not the only species considered a gourmet's delicacy - other related frogs are also caught for this reason.

The Marsh Frog (*R. ridibunda*) is a native of mainland Europe, although it was first introduced to Britain about 1935, when a number of individuals were released in the area of the Romney Marshes in Kent and Sussex. The original ancestors of the British strain which has subsequently evolved were believed to have come from Hungary. As a result, the British form is relatively dark in colour — races from southern Europe are more greenish than those found in the eastern part of their range. It is greenish-olive overall with black markings. The vocal sacs of the males are greyish. It is a fairly noisy species, croaking readily, especially during the breeding season.

These are gregarious frogs, naturally occurring in groups, and spend much of their time in the water, although they can often be seen in a pond sitting on lily pads, or resting nearby, with their heads visible above the water. The Marsh Frog is the largest species occurring in Britain, reaching a size of 15 cm (6 ins).

Another noisy frog which has been introduced to new localities is the Bullfrog (*R. catesbeiana*) found widely throughout the United States. They are extremely vocal, and fairly solitary when adult. Bullfrogs are hearty carnivores, and will not hesitate to eat their own offspring. They can be sexed without difficulty, since the ear opening or timpanum of these frogs is much smaller in the case of the female, corresponding approximately to the size of the eye. Their tadpoles may take two years to metamorphose, by which time they can be 7.5 cm (3 ins) or so in length, having lost their tails.

A closely-related American species is the Green Frog (*R. clamitans*), which resembles the Bullfrog, although it is much smaller and quite gregarious by nature. The Pickerel Frog (*R. palustris*) has an attractive appearance, but also possesses a poisonous skin secretion, and so should not be included in the pond if possible. The Leopard Frog (*R. pipiens*) is another common species though, ranging over most of the United States, which will do well under pond conditions.

Toads

Toads differ from frogs by having shorter legs, so they crawl rather than hop. In addition, their skins are not smooth but warty in appearance. Two species occur in Britain, but will only be seen in the pond when breeding.

The Common Toad (*Bufo bufo*) reaches 15 cm (6 ins), with females being bigger than males. It is brownish in colour, with a copper or golden-coloured eye. Mainly active at night, the Common Toad spends much of its time hidden in a specific spot during the day. It hibernates on land, in a suitable burrow, from October onwards, depending on the temperature.

The Natterjack Toad (*B. calamita*) is a rare species, but instantly recognisable by the yellow stripe running down its back. The body coloration is green. Its call can often be heard in the evening, and it is largely nocturnal in its habits. The Natterjack Toad is a fast mover, quite able to run over short distances, and likely to be encountered in sandy areas close to water.

In common with other toads, it lays its eggs in long chains, rather than as a mass, like frogs. They nevertheless have a similar life cycle. A single female may produce as many as a thousand eggs, which should hatch in about a week to yield the larval form, known as tadpoles. Those which survive and metamorphose into toads will themselves be mature in about three years.

Toads are surprisingly long-lived creatures, and can survive for two decades or more under favourable conditions. They generally feed only on livefoods, such as earthworms. It is important that they are able to leave the pond after entering the water. Unlike newts, which can often climb a vertical surface without difficulty, frogs and toads may encounter more difficulty under such conditions.

Care of frogs and toads

Apart from their interesting habits, the inclusion of frogs or toads in a pond will help to boost their numbers in the area. Some species are showing a serious decline in numbers, as their habitats are drained or polluted. They require virtually no attention at all compared to fish, although appropriate livefoods can be offered. Anurans are generally harmless in the pond, although occasionally an over-zealous male may grab a passing fish in a mistaken mating attempt. Such an event is rare, however, as most fish are too nimble to be caught in this way.

The easiest means of introducing these creatures to a pond is to obtain some spawn during the spring, although fish may consume this along with any resultant tadpoles which do hatch. Young survivors will eat a variety of food and grow quite rapidly.

The length of time taken for the tadpoles to emerge as miniature adults varies according to the species concerned. Their back legs become apparent first, followed by their front limbs. As they start to breathe air, they must have easy access out of the pond, and preferably cover nearby on land where they can hide. Here they will take whiteworms and similar livefoods and hopefully will return to breed themselves in subsequent years.

When handling amphibians, they must be treated in the same way as fish, and only restrained with wet hands. Damage to their skin may precipitate an outbreak of red leg, which is a bacterial disease resulting from infection with *Aeromonas hydrophilia*. This condition causes a reddening of the skin, coupled with loss of appetite and swelling of the limbs. Treatment is difficult, although antibiotics given directly may be of assistance. Tetracyclines should not be used in the water for therapeutic purposes though since they irritate amphibians' skin.

Terrapins in the pond

A pond may be considered an ideal environment for keeping terrapins during the summer months. Undeniably it will give them much more space than could be available in an aquarium, as well as access to sunlight, which is an important appetite stimulus, and will help to prevent the disease known as 'soft shell'. If terrapins are to be kept in this way, though, then the pond must be adapted for the purpose. In addition, because of their predatory natures, these reptiles cannot be kept satisfactorily alongside fish.

A central island in the pond, where the terrapins can readily climb out to walk and sunbathe, is recommended, or alternatively there must be sufficient space allowed for this around the edge of the pond. A perimeter fence, set into the ground, will be required as a surround so that the terrapins cannot wander off into the garden and get lost.

Terrapins are basically carnivorous in their feeding habits, and should be fed accordingly. It is inadvisable to feed raw meat directly in the pond, however, because any surplus will rapidly sour the water. Worms of various types, freshwater shrimps and even the irradiated prepared foodstuffs mentioned previously will keep terrapins in good health with variety being particularly important.

No terrapins occur naturally in Britain, although the European Pond species (*Emys orbicularis*) and the Spanish Terrapin (*Clemmys leprosa*), found on the European mainland, are sometimes imported. Many small hatchling Red-eared Terrapins (*Chrysemys scripta*) are imported each year from North America. They are basically green, with a yellowish underpart to the shell, and have a characteristic red stripe extending back from the eyes on either side of the head. These terrapins are not suitable for ponds, as they must be kept in heated water, at a minimum temperature of 24°C (75°F).

Larger specimens, with a shell length of about 12.5 cm (5 ins) can, however, be kept outside during the summer. A check should be made to ensure that they are eating, and in the autumn they must be brought inside and kept in an aquarium over the winter. In their natural state, terrapins may hibernate by burrowing into the mud at the bottom of the pond, but obviously this is neither practical nor necessary in artificial surroundings. The health of the terrapins will not suffer if they are housed properly for the duration of the winter, nor will their lifespan be affected.

Snails

The inclusion of snails in the pond is a controversial topic. Although they have a reputation for being useful scavengers, their numbers can increase rapidly and, as with their terrestrial counterparts, aquatic snails will often damage plants growing in the pond. They also add to the general level of contamination by creating further detrius, and may also introduce fish parasites, since certain species are intermediate hosts in some life cycles.

There are 36 species of aquatic snails known in Britain. The Great Pond Snail (*Lymnaea stagnalis*) is the largest, with a conical shell which can be 5 cm (2 ins) or more in length. The shell itself is brownish and tapers to a point, in common with other members of this genus. It cannot withdraw its tentacles. These snails are omnivorous, and will attack fry and even newts, as well as inanimate feeding matter. They reproduce by means of eggs, which are laid in elongated clumps protected in jelly on plants and stonework.

The *Planorbis* snails are commonly referred to as Ramshorn species. They take this description from the shape of their shells, which are coiled. Their size varies from the minute *P. orista*, having a shell only 3 mm (⅛ inch) in diameter, to the giant form, *P. corneus* which may reach 2.5 cm (1 inch) across. The coloration of the red form results from the presence of haemaglobin, and since no actual colour pigment is present, the snail appears reddish.

The bivalves are related to snails, but form a separate class within the phylum Mollusca. Their shells consist of two pieces bound together by a tight ligament. They spend much of their lives partially buried in mud, although they communicate with their immediate environment by means of two siphons.

The Swan Mussel (*Anodonta cygnea*) is vital for the successful breeding of Bitterling (*Rhodeus amarus*) as mentioned previously. It is a relatively large mussel, growing to about 20 cm (6 ins) in size, and has a greenish-brown shell. Females produce eggs which are fertilised through the inhalation siphon, and subsequently stored in the brood pouches. The resulting larvae, called *glochidia*, are expelled through the exhalant (outlet) siphon into the water, complete with miniature shells and a sharp tooth. They also possess a thread-like structure, referred to as the byssus, which operates the two valves, thus enabling the glochidia to swim. The immature mussels are parasitic at this stage in their life cycle and must locate a fish. Once attached, they embed into its skin by means of the tooth, and form a cyst. After about three months, during which time they will have been nourished by their host's blood, the mussels emerge, complete with a new shell, and assume a free-living existence. Suitable containers will be required if these mussels are to be included in the pond.

Insect life

A wide variety of insects can be observed both around and in the pond. Some of these creatures are potentially harmful to fish, and should be excluded if possible. The various beetles fit into this category, since the majority are carnivorous by nature. One of the largest is *Dytiscus marginalis*, known as the Giant Diving Beetle, which can reach a size of 3.7 cm (1½ ins). These beetles are blackish-brown in colour, with yellow markings on their upper surface, and yellow underparts beneath. Their eggs are sometimes laid at the water's surface, or hidden in plants which have been chewed for this purpose. The larvae are equally ferocious when they hatch, and remain at this stage for a year. Prey is seized with their powerful jaws and injected with digestive juices. The immature beetles leave the water to pupate, localising in any damp patches around the side of the pond.

Although Great Diving Beetles can be introduced carelessly in the company of plants or livefood, they are also capable of flight, in search of new areas of water. There are other similar carnivorous species, including the Two-spotted (*Agabus bipustulatus*) characterised by two red dots normally present on the head. *Colymbetes fuscus* resembles the Great Diving Beetle but is smaller, and lacks the yellow markings on its upperparts.

In the case of the Great Silver Water Beetle (*Hydrous piceus*), the larval stage only is strictly carnivorous. The adults, which can grow to 5 cm (2 ins), are jet black in colour and omnivorous in their feeding habits. They frequent densely planted water, and actually lay their eggs in cocoons spun of silk which float on the water's surface.

Water-boatmen are often seen in quiet stretches of water moving with their characteristic jerky rowing motion, from which they are named. They spend much of their lives upside down, since they both swim and rest at the surface in this position, with their abdomen uppermost to enable them to breathe air. Two forms are recognised, with the Lesser (*Corixa punctata*) being distinguished since its middle legs are developed to resemble the oars, whereas in the case of the Greater (*Notonecta glauca*) its main thrust comes from the powerful elongated hind limbs. Like the water beetles, these insects are highly predatory and will attack fish. They lay eggs in plants, and the eggs hatch into pale miniatures of the adults, apart from their red eyes.

The Water Scorpion (*Nipa cinerea*) is greyish in colour, with its elongated shape being reminiscent of a dead leaf. It can be up to 2.5 cm (1 inch) in length. It has no sting, but possesses extremely strong front limbs modified to grasp prey, which it consumes with its powerful jaws. Water Scorpions are commonly found around the edge of the pond, often disguised in mud. A similar insect is the Water Stick Insect, (*Ranatra linearis*) which has a reddish body, and is generally bigger than the Water Scorpion.

Dragonflies make an attractive sight, buzzing around the pond on a summer's day. The Emperor Dragonfly (*Anax imperator*) is the largest British species, reaching a size of 7.5 cm (3 ins) or so. It is an irridescent blue in colour, with big, green eyes and, in contrast to other species, often frequents still waters. The larval stage of the dragonfly is, however, a rather sluggish predator, living in the pond, which waits for prey to approach before grabbing it with its strong mouthparts.

Another aerial insect whose aggressive larvae live in water is the Alder Fly (*Sialis lutaria*). Females lay their eggs around the pond's perimeter, and the resulting larvae live in the mud for two years. They may grow to 2.5 cm (1 inch) in size, and prey on creatures smaller than themselves.

Hydra, in contrast, lives exclusively in water. It is a minute jelly-like organism, often introduced to the pond in the company of aquatic livefood. The stinging tentacles of *Hydra* serve to paralyse small prey, such as fry, but if disturbed, it can contract down to an inconspicuous blob, in order to escape detection.

Microscopic organisms

While the above gives brief details about some of the most common predatory insects present in ponds, there will be an even greater number of microscopic creatures inhabiting the pond and preying on each other. Studying these with the aid of a basic microscope can be a fascinating pastime. Although it will probably not be possible to identify all the organisms, a vast range of colour and shapes can be seen.

In order to make a slide for study, a pipette, slide and coverslip will be required. Using the pipette, a sample of pond

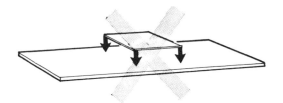

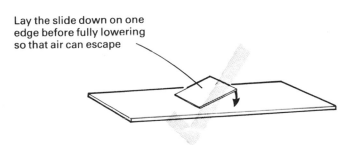

Lay the slide down on one
edge before fully lowering
so that air can escape

Preparation of a microscope slide to avoid air bubbles

water can be drawn up, with just a single drop being transferred to the centre of the slide. This will contain plenty of organisms, and too much water will simply flood the slide when the coverslip is placed on top.

Irrespective of whether it is square or circular, the coverslip needs to be applied carefully, to prevent air lodging beneath, reducing the field of vision when the slide is mounted under the microscope. It should be placed at the edge of a drop, making actual contact with the water, before being lowered carefully downwards. If the cover-slip is just dropped horizontally, much more air is liable to be trapped as a result. The slide should be viewed through the lowest power magnification at first. It is then possible to move up to a high power to focus on an organism of particular interest, having obtained an overall picture of the field of vision.

Maintenance and expansion

Having been set up in the spring, the pond should be well-established by the summer. Young fish may be evident, in amongst the growing plants. This is also the time of year though when the predators listed in the previous chapter are likely to be apparent, and must be removed before they can cause harm. Their size is not an adequate reflection of the damage which they can inflict, since the Great Diving Beetle, for example, may attack fish as large as 15 cm (6 ins) in length.

An autumn clean-up

The pond will go into a decline during the autumn, with the plants showing signs of dying back, while the fish become sluggish at the approach of winter, although their appetites will be briefly rekindled beforehand. It is a good idea to empty and clean the pond in late autumn, netting all the fish beforehand. Those which are under 5 cm (2 ins) long will have to be kept inside during the winter. Dead or decaying plants should be removed, along with other debris, so that the remaining fish can be returned to a clean environment for the winter.

Winter care

It is often beneficial to cover all or part of the pond, which should help to prevent the water freezing over completely. Such a cover does not need to be an elaborate structure, but must be made from non-toxic materials. Various designs are possible, but the framework itself needs to be sufficiently strong to withstand the weight of snow which may accumulate on its surfaces. The sides must slope away from the pond, so that snow and debris cannot fall into the water. Special horticultural plastic is ideal for covering the framework, since it enables sunlight to penetrate to the water beneath. This sheeting should be fixed to the frame with battening on top, so it will not be ripped or torn by a strong wind. Protective coverings of this type are especially favoured by koi keepers, but will benefit all fish.

If left uncovered, the water surface is likely to freeze, but ice will only form to a maximum depth of about 45 cm (18 ins) even under really severe conditions. It will be necessary to make a hole in the ice, though, so that noxious gases can escape as well as lessening the force on the pond walls, since the water will have expanded on freezing. It is vital not to launch an assault on the ice with a chisel or hammer though, since the shock waves of the blows transmitted to the water under the ice are likely to concuss and probably kill the fish.

The safest alternative is to hold a saucepan containing boiling water on top of the ice, which will gradually melt, depending on its thickness. Another method which can be used to maintain a hole in the ice is a pond heater, although these should not raise the temperature so high that the fish are brought out of their torpid state prematurely. It is also possible to float a piece of wood on the surface at night when the water is likely to freeze over. The wood is then removed the following morning, leaving a hole in the ice. A plug of material can alternatively be inserted in an established opening to keep the water below from freezing.

A small volume of water can be siphoned out of the pond at this stage, enabling a thin layer of air to be in contact with the water under the ice. Any snow which accumulates above must be brushed off at regular intervals, so that light can penetrate to the plants. They will then be able to continue photosynthesising, giving off oxygen in the process. By way of contrast, if the weather remains very mild, causing the fish to remain active, they should be offered daphnia as food. If not eaten, these crustaceans will continue living in the water, and do not pollute it, although they will require oxygen like the fish themselves.

Spring revival

At the onset of spring, the plants in the pond are likely to benefit from attention. Lilies, for example, may need dividing with a sharp knife. Pieces of the tuber showing shoots should be kept, while the oldest part must be discarded, otherwise it is liable to rot away. Marginals also may have outgrown their containers and therefore need to be split up. Rhizomes of irises can be cut in a similar way to water-lilies. Oxygenators should start growing rapidly in the spring and additional pieces can be rooted as required.

A watch should be kept in the spring for blanketweed, which is a conspicuous form of alga. It grows in thick strands and may rapidly clog up other plants. This algae should be removed by pulling clumps out, cautiously using either a stick or rake for the purpose. Other related species of alga may cloud the water in the early spring, until the lilies and other plants are re-established again. Some pond-keepers favour a partial water change at this time of year, replacing perhaps a third of the total volume with fresh, mature tapwater. Electrical apparatus should also be checked and overhauled as required, in preparation for further use during the warmer months ahead.

Streams and waterfalls

The addition of artificial running water to an established pond set-up can be conveniently carried out in the spring, with the choice of materials available similar to those used initially for the construction of the pond. In this instance, though, fibreglass units are extremely useful. A significant depth for the channel is not important, and indeed a relatively shallow stream is preferable since it will create a more natural effect. It is important that the steps of the fall are not made too deep, otherwise excessive water may be lost by splashing. There must also be adequate water in the pond to supply the water course, which may restrict its length.

Fibreglass units should first be set out roughly in place, enabling them to be adjusted as necessary. They will require a firm base of well-trodden soil, and the sides can be filled in once they are in place. Care is required to ensure that no earth can be splashed in the watercourse during heavy rain, since this will ultimately be washed into the pond. At the top of the elevation, where the water enters, pumped up via a pipe from the pond, plants and large stones can be used to good effect to disguise the water's source.

Pond liners are another alternative which can form the base of streams and falls, although under these conditions, construction can present additional difficulties. The shape of the water course must be dug out, taking care to remove any sharp projections which could puncture the liner. The resulting series of steps may require additional support to prevent the soil collapsing. Once the liner is in place, slabs can be positioned both horizontally and vertically for this purpose. It is vital that the liner itself is laid taut over the contours of the excavation, as any sagging at this stage will result in discrete channels of water being formed later. Stones again can be used around the perimeter to obscure the liner, while shallow falls are preferable for the same reason.

Concrete is the most flexible material for constructing a water course, yet it must be laid correctly, as described previously, for building the pond itself. A solid base of hardcore will again be required, with concrete laid on top of this to form a curved channel, when viewed in cross-section. A cement rendering will be necessary as before, and it is essential to deal with the free lime, once the cement has dried. A chemical covering to achieve this aim is likely to be necessary, especially if the water course is constructed after the fish are installed in the pond below.

Bog gardens

A bog garden can easily be designed as part of the water course, or independently around the pond. The chosen area should be excavated to about 30 cm (1 foot) in depth, and a pool liner or polythene set in the hollow. The soil, mixed with peat which will help to retain water, is then replaced on top. After a thorough soaking, the area can be planted with the required plants. When it rains, water will be trapped in the soil, and only perhaps during the summer will it be necessary to keep the area artificially moist. Many marginal plants will do well under such wet conditions, while various other species can be included.

Repairs

Damage to the pond will soon become evident, as the water-level declines noticeably. Evaporative loss of water from the pond is likely to be a much more gradual process. A tear in a PVC liner is easy to repair by sticking a patch of the material over the damaged area, always allowing adequate overlap. A special glue should be used for this purpose, with the patch being held firmly in place for a few minutes afterwards. The bonding surfaces must be dry though, and so it is likely that the pond will have to be emptied beforehand. The adhesive will set rapidly so that water can be introduced again after about an hour. A similar method is used for the repair of butyl ponds, and repair kits for both types of liner can be obtained. It is useful to have the appropriate kit to hand for an emergency. Polythene liners cannot be repaired satisfactorily, and must be discarded.

Glass fibre ponds are not difficult to patch effectively using a kit as available for repairing damaged car bodies. Concrete is the most difficult material to renovate once it is cracked and leaking. Such damage can result from the effects of frost or subsidence, especially on a clay soil. The best means of rendering the pond water-tight again is to use a liner on the inner surface, thus creating a second pool within the confines of the first. This is a reliable method, even if the ground expands or contracts again. Properly constructed, though, the majority of ponds will give years of enjoyment without any problems.

Bibliography

There are many different aspects relating to ponds, and for more detailed information on specific topics, reference to the following titles may be useful:

Alderton, D.   *Tortoises and Terrapins* (Saiga Publishing)
Axelrod, H.R.   *Koi of the World* (TFH)
Bartrum, D.   *Water in the Garden* (John Gifford)
Boarder, A.   *Coldwater Fishkeeping* (Buckley Press)
Clegg, J.   *The Observer's Book of Pond Life* (Frederick Warne)
Heritage, W.   *Ponds and Water Gardens* (Blandford)
Hervey, G.F. &
  Hems, J.   *The Goldfish* (Faber and Faber)
Masters, C.O.   *Encyclopedia of Livefoods* (TFH)
Masters, C.O.   *Encyclopedia of Water-lilies* (TFH)
Orme, F.W.   *Fancy Goldfish Culture* (Saiga Publishing)
Orme, F.W.   *Cyclopaedia of Coldwater Fish and Pond Life* (Saiga Publishing)
Perry, F.   *The Garden Pool* (David and Charles)
Sherwell-Cooper,
  W.E.   *Rock Gardens and Pools* (Drake Publishing Inc.)
Stodola, J.   *Encyclopedia of Water Plants* (TFH)

The following journals also often contain articles of interest to the pond-keeper:

Practical Fishkeeping
Aquarist and Pond-keeper

Index

Figures in italics refer to illustrations.